Eyes that See paints a vivid picture of the Christian faith. I find myself both horribly devastated by the tremendous loss in this story but also deeply moved by the incredible love and faith, and midst of that I am mysteriously drawn to live life d faithfully myself. Judson's story needed ne, needed to read it.

—Steve Porter
Associate Professor,
gy, Biola University

This is a poignant ess through profound suffering and i. a courageous journey that challenges f refining faith, transforming hope, an

Executive Pastor,

Christina Levasheff is an incredible 'cu of the heart' and this story is a vulnerably-raw, po , and moving experience! She connects and compels the reader to engage her life, where they find both comfort and hope in every written expression, along with permission to feel and express pain. *Eyes that See* is an invitation into a unique and precious journey of suffering and determination to seek after God's own heart.

—Rinette Mills
Director of Women's Ministries, Faith Community Church

Where affliction and pain reside, we find hope in the story of Judson. This soul-wrenching account of one small yet incredibly-significant life takes you on a journey of unwavering faith.

—Darlene Schacht
Founder & Editor,
Christian Women Online Magazine

I feel like Judson's story should be required reading for everyone. There's so much there for all of us to learn and ponder about the value of life here on earth, life in heaven, faith, prayer, suffering, love, and so much else. It's heartbreaking but amazing reading.

—*David E. Snyder, La Mirada, CA*

Finding Judson's story was like being thrown a life preserver. I was barely holding on. The Lord spoke clearly to me through his life, and I will never forget who my Savior is again."

—*Elaina M. Avalos, Hubert, NC*

These parents lived through something that no parent wants to even imagine. I can't begin to describe how I felt, laughing on one paragraph, crying on the next, sobbing on another, only to return to a smile yet again. Judson's story is bringing people like me to stop and be thankful for what God has given us and to see the good in the worst of situations.

—*Seaandra Pearson, Summerfield, FL*

Judson's story gives us the model of true Christianity: Remain faithful through it *all*, even when he takes away.

—*Joshua Klinge, Orange, CA*

This story is told so sincerely, heart-wrenchingly, and yet with such faith.

—*Rachael Boer, Gaithersburg, MD*

Judson has left an imprint on my heart—forever!

—*Shannon Pinkard, Boulder City, NV*

My faith has been encouraged by Judson's story to see the Gospel provide real hope in the midst of suffering.

—*Adam Groza, Fort Worth, TX*

This story of faith has challenged my heart to keep trusting, keep hoping, and keep clinging to the goodenss of our Lord.

—*Sue Lee, Irvine, CA*

Eyes that See

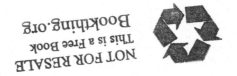

Eyes that See

Judson's Story of Hope in Suffering

CHRISTINA ADELSECK LEVASHEFF

WITH A FOREWORD BY EMILIE BARNES

TATE PUBLISHING & *Enterprises*

Published by Tate Publishing & Enterprises, LLC
127 E. Trade Center Terrace | Mustang, Oklahoma 73064 USA
1.888.361.9473 | www.tatepublishing.com

Tate Publishing is committed to excellence in the publishing industry. The company reflects the philosophy established by the founders, based on Psalm 68:11,
"The Lord gave the word and great was the company of those who published it."

Book design copyright © 2009 by Tate Publishing, LLC. All rights reserved.
Cover design by Leah LeFlore
Interior design by Jeff Fisher

Published in the United States of America

ISBN: 978-1-60799-993-5
1. Biography & Autobiography, Personal Memoirs
2. Religion, Christian Life, Inspirational
11.06.06

Dedication

This book is dedicated to my beautiful daughter, Jessie, our "joy in the morning." Your life is a miracle, bringing such light and joy to the world. Indeed, you are a huge blessing, just like your brother!

Acknowledgments

In many ways, this book was inadvertently written; it grew organically out of a desire to update family, friends, and even compassionate strangers about Judson's journey; and because they cared enough to know the depths of our experience, I kept writing. This book was born out of the love we received from so many. We are eternally grateful to those who supported us through our darkest valley.

Though I may have been the one writing, my husband, Drake, inspired much of what is contained in these pages, whether it was through our conversations or simply observing his steadfast trust as he battled for the life of his son. Drake's fortitude, persistence, tenderness, and grace through unimaginable circumstances stimulated my faith in the Lord, and I am grateful to be walking through life with such an honorable man.

I want to thank all our family, especially Chuck and Marsha Adelseck, Stan and Lori Levasheff, and Danielle and Marty Jones, who were there for us at the drop of a hat and tirelessly sacrificed for us during

Judson's illness. Furthermore, Sarah Hegenbart Bobar has become like a sister through this process as she tenderly loved and gave of her heart to our precious boy, her little buddy.

We would not have survived this season without the support of our church family. Grace Fellowship Church offered us tangible expressions of God's love and beautifully reflected the gospel and God's design for the church through our tragedy. We are continually grateful for our church body, especially Rachel Toberty, who has given so much of her time and heart to our family and taken "Jessie Girl" under her wing, along with Melissa Guzman, who sweetly cared for Judson at church and in our home.

God also mobilized his people worldwide to reach out to our family, and it is through all the notes of encouragement, prayers, gifts, meals, financial support, or other unexpected blessings that our Father has used to make his abundant love known to us. Thank you to *everyone* who has supported us in these ways!

Many people, unknowingly at the time, contributed letters to this book, and I am grateful for their permission to use their thoughts. I also deeply appreciate all the people who took the time to endorse this book, along with the many strangers who read *Eyes that See* while it was online and gave me permission to quote their responses to Jud's story.

I'd like to offer a special thanks to Emilie Barnes, who believed in this story and was willing to present this book to people in the publishing field and support me as a new author by writing a foreword.

Judson is one of *many* young children who lose their lives to awful diseases every day. We are blessed that Judson's story is being told but also recognize that each parent wants their child to be remembered and cherished, and we hope this book can help bring awareness to all the children who have lost their lives, especially to leukodystrophies. I am grateful to the "Band of Mothers" I have met online who have walked a similar journey, and the Hunter's Hope Foundation that is committed to increasing awareness and treatments for Krabbe, expanding the likelihood of early detection for many disorders through Universal Newborn Screening (UNBS), while supporting families afflicted by leukodystrophy diseases.

Lastly, I wish that I still had my amazing little boy who touched me each day with his sweet spirit, sharp mind, and playful antics. I wish this book did not exist. But I am eternally grateful for his life, which taught me so much, and I pray it may touch you too.

Table of Contents

Foreword

Periodically you stumble upon a gifted new author with a compelling story, and you know you have found a treasure. It did not take me long to realize that *Eyes that See: Judson's Story of Hope in Suffering* by Christina Levasheff is one such treasure.

A long-time friend of mine who is part of the same church family as Christina gave me a copy of *Eyes that See.* My husband, Bob, and I picked up the manuscript to peruse it while in flight to the East Coast but soon discovered it was a book we could not put down. We read the entire story during our travels and were very moved by this journey of unfailing faith.

Christina writes as though we were talking over a cup of our favorite tea. She is sharing her intimate, personal thoughts as she experiences every parent and grandparent's worst nightmare. The smooth flow of her writing allows us to easily enter into her family's faith, love, hope, and joy during their intense struggles as their beloved son, Jud, battles an awful disease.

We quickly see that Judson is an extraordinary boy. Even at two years old, he was speaking truth from his heart and revealing Jesus to everyone around him.

As his body deteriorated, he still offered love and encouragement and kept the family hopeful. He had a real zest for life, even in great suffering, and always shared his smile.

In the beginning of this book, there is an important paragraph where Christina writes how God whispers in her ear: "Judson is special. I have great plans for him, but I will care for him. He is special." I believe that everyone who picks up this book will quickly see that Judson certainly is special, and God wants to use him and the faithfulness of his family to help each of us have eyes that see and trust the Lord in adversity.

David, the psalmist, writes in Psalm 30:5 (NASB), "Weeping may last for the night, but a shout of joy comes in the morning." Our dear Levasheff family, we look forward to the day you will hear the shouts of joy!

—*Emilie Barnes*

Emilie Barnes is a best-selling author with over sixty-five books including, *A Journey through Cancer, Safe in the Father's Hands,* and *Heal My Heart, Lord.* She is also an internationally acclaimed speaker and founder of "More Hours in My Day" seminars. Emilie is listed as one of the 100 Christian Women Who Changed the 20th Century.

Prologue

•   •   •

"Daddy, why are you crying?"

I watched my husband, Drake, tenderly reach out a trembling hand toward our almost two-and-a-half-year-old son as tears streamed down his face.

"All the problems we've been having have been hard, Judson. We want you to be able to see and walk again."

In that moment, Jud began quoting, word for word, the story of Job from his toddler Bible[1], "One day a man ran to Job. 'Your children and animals have died,' he said. Then Job got sores all over him."

Drake began to cry harder.

"Do you want me to hold you, Daddy?"

"That would be great, Jud, but why don't you finish eating first."

Jud continued with the story of Job. "Did Job get angry at God? No! 'God gave me all I had,' said Job. 'I will still love him.'"

•   •   •

As the weight of truth expressed in Judson's words settled in our hearts, we became convinced that our beautiful son had uncommon spiritual understanding, and it would be vital for us to listen closely to all God might choose to convey through our recently vision-impaired child; Judson could see God … we wanted to develop eyes that could see him too.

Contained in these pages is how the Lord chose to reveal himself through the story of our dearly loved son, Judson, whose body, having been healthy and whole for the first years of his life, began to rapidly deteriorate just prior to turning two and a half. His story may be remarkable, but inherent in his journey, and our journey along with him, is deep suffering and pain—the kind of affliction that redefines one's life and faith forever. And with the onset of this adversity in our family came a choice: what lens will we use to view God in our heartache?

I began to recognize that the Lord was calling me to embrace the vision of life found in the story of Job as articulated by my blind and suffering son. I needed to see my circumstances through the lens of God's character and grace, despite the hardship, affliction, and pain. I had to make a conscious choice every day to keep my eyes open for whatever the Lord wanted to teach me through this precious little boy entrusted to my care. Judson's story became a considerable journey of faith and hope, coupled with tremendous agony and ultimately an underlying call to trust my heavenly Father in *everything*.

I invite you to walk with me on this road of faith and hope in suffering conveyed through our sweet little man as experienced by us, his parents. The following chapter will allow you to meet Judson, while the subsequent chapters are a chronological compilation of letters, personal reflections, correspondence, and thoughts from others, along with stories of Jud, all written throughout this journey.

They are dated and were actually composed on the given dates during his season of affliction. They tell Jud's saga the way it was revealed to those who walked this path of pain with us as it occurred. You might laugh, cry, and hope with us, but most of all it is our desire that Judson's life will challenge you to view your own life from a new perspective.

May the story of our suddenly blind little boy give you *Eyes that See*.

Meet Judson

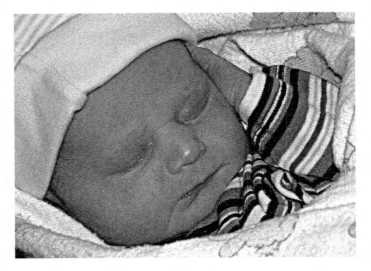

Children are a gift of the Lord.

Psalm 127:3 NASB

•   •   •

Judson Drake Levasheff was born on Christmas Eve 2004.

He was extremely healthy, with eyes that were literally wide-open and already tracking with the world. We rejoiced in this incredible gift of life, our first child, and immediately fell in love. Yet we did not fully realize what an amazing treasure we were cradling in our arms.

During the first year of Judson's life, our home was filled with sounds of cooing, vocalizing, and also screaming and crying. Judson definitely made his presence known.

One afternoon when Judson was about eight months old, he began crying uncontrollably. I started rocking him, and tears began to stream down my face; I was powerless to comfort him. In that broken moment, I sensed God whispering in my ear, "Judson is *special*. I have *great* plans for him, but *I* will care for him. He is special."

As a proud, first-time mother, I began to believe God must have meant Judson was "special" when his many sounds became intelligible earlier than one might expect. His vocabulary was bursting at fourteen months of age, and by eighteen months old he was clearly articulating his thoughts.

At the same time that his speech and vocabulary were developing, he had a growing love for the park nearby our home. He delighted in climbing, running, swinging, and sliding, while also enjoying the company of other children.

Judson's love for automobiles was also emerging, putting his acute memory and ability to make fine distinctions on display. Jud was never just playing with a "truck;" he was playing with a "Land Rover" or an "SUV" or an "Army Jeep."

Jud loved singing too. He could be heard in the midst of any day belting out, "The Itsy, Bitsy ~~Spider~~ Elephant"[2] (with a grin, because he knew it was too big) or "Step by Step" by Rich Mullins.[3] A highlight was when he entertained Drake's colleagues at a 2006 Christmas party with his rendition of "The B-I-B-L-E."[4]

While Drake and I marveled at how well he spoke, his ability to express himself also gave us the privilege of knowing his young heart. Judson's speech revealed a tenderhearted, bright, humorous boy with a sweet spirit, who loved others and seemed to have a heart inclined toward God.

One of the most important developments in Judson's young life was the arrival of his sister, Jessie Lynn, when he was nineteen months old. From the day we welcomed Jessie into our home, Judson exhibited great care for her; he would bring her his favorite toys to play with and shower her with hugs and kisses. He loved having Jessie around and always wanted to ensure that she was included. Whether in the car or double stroller, Jud often reached out and gently held her hand (you can imagine what this meant to us as parents!).

Drake and I have long been convinced that children are not simply a gift to their parents, but a gift from God to the world. Our task as Christian parents, at least as we see it, is to partner with our Father to give our children to God's church and the world, that they would be a blessing.

So from the time our little baby boy began developing in my womb, we prayed many things; but most of all, similar to God's promise to Abraham, we prayed that this little person, Judson Drake Levasheff, whom the Lord commended to us, would be a blessing to others.

> I will bless you; I will make your name great,
> and you will be a blessing.
>
> *Genesis* 12:2

What we did not foresee was the manner by which God would choose to answer this prayer.

Month One:
My World is Crumbling

Letter 1: Wednesday, June 13, 2007

Dear family and friends,

We have very quickly found ourselves in a position of concern for Judson's health.

A few weeks ago, I noticed that Jud was stumbling a little while walking. I didn't think much of it at the time. However, as days passed, it seemed to be getting worse.

I took Jud to see the doctor last Thursday to discuss his recent propensity to stumble and fall. Because Judson displayed some cold symptoms, the doctor surmised that his wobbly walk was probably related to an infection affecting his balance and would quickly subside.

The next couple days it continued to worsen, and then we began to notice that Jud was starting to over-reach or under-reach for his target when he used his hands to grasp things.

Today we finally got back in to see the doctor and have since found ourselves in a whirlwind. Because it appears as though Jud can't "see" things when he reaches for them, the doctor wanted to rule out any problems with his eyes before proceeding with concerns that it may be an issue related to his brain. We were sent to an ophthalmologist, who determined that Jud's eyes are functioning perfectly. However, that has led the doctors to believe Judson may have some type of neurological disorder affecting his eyesight and balance.

They have scheduled an emergency MRI for him tomorrow morning. We have also been referred to a pediatric neurologist.

As you can imagine, our minds are racing with fears. Unfortunately, information on the Internet has only heightened those fears (I have since stopped looking at the Internet).

Please pray with us. Please pray that the MRI will go smoothly tomorrow—sedation will be required because he is so young (this, in and of itself, is very hard for me). Please pray that the neurologist will be able to quickly gain insight into the cause of Jud's symptoms. Please pray that the cause is not of a serious nature. Please pray for physical and emotional strength for Drake and me. Please pray for healing. Jud is so young, and the potential issues all seem very serious.

Thank you for your love and prayers,
Christina (on behalf of Drake too)

P.S. Jud (twenty-nine months) and Jessie (almost ten months) have been so much fun as they grow in age and character. We feel so blessed! Many of you have not seen them or pictures of them in a while, so I have enclosed a recent picture. I also thought you might enjoy seeing a video of Jud singing "The Star Spangled Banner" (viewable at www.StoryOfJudson. com).

Letter 2: Thursday, June 14

Dear family and friends,

Thank you so much for the outpouring of love, support, and prayers!

It has been a very difficult morning; we were told when we arrived at the hospital that Jud would be rushed to neuro-surgery in Los Angeles after the MRI if they found a brain tumor. As you can imagine, our hearts sank, and the next hours were all the more challenging!

The MRI is over (not an easy experience with a two-year-old), and Judson is home with us, napping right now.

We are so thankful and relieved that he does not have a brain tumor. However, they did find problems in the "white mat-ter" of his brain. This is consistent with the symptoms that have been observed. The next step is to determine the root cause; though the neurologist indicated that the situation is not acute, most of the possibilities are still very serious.

The hardest part for us right now is the unknown, and unfortunately, we will not be able to meet with the pediatric neurologist for another four days; he is on vacation. There-fore, we won't have any more information until then.

Many of you have asked about Jessie and meals. We are so thankful to have had Drake's parents caring for Jessie these last two days, and my mom and dad are now staying with us to lend a helping hand. We certainly feel surrounded with love and will let you know if specific needs arise. I am hop-ing we can get some semblance of "life as normal" the next couple days and then deal with new information as it comes to us.

Having children has made us vulnerable to a whole new set of challenges and pains, but God is good—seen especially through the love of his people. He made Judson and loves Judson even more than we do. We are just so thankful that he has entrusted this little guy to our care!

Please continue to pray for us. Please pray for the healing of Jud's body and for the neurologist to have great insight into diagnosis and treatment. Please continue to pray for Drake and me to have emotional and physical strength during this time, along with wisdom and patience. Lastly, please pray that the strains and stresses of the situation bring a deepening of our love for one another and for God, who graciously works all things out for his purposes.

We cannot begin to tell you what your support means to us.

Love,
Christina (on behalf of Drake too)

Journal Entry: Thursday, June 14

Eyes to See

Today has been one of the most challenging days I've probably ever had. On the flipside, many blessings were present. Beauty and grace flowed abundantly.

I want eyes to see. I want eyes to see the goodness of God that surrounds us—especially in trials.

Today we experienced God's grace come from a "random" doctor who took us under his wing and advocated for us in a time of great uncertainty. Grace came from the knowing, caring smiles of people from our church who were there when we rolled Jud in for his MRI. It came from Jud's cousins and aunt, who waited outside the hospital with balloons and gifts for him. It came from Drake's family who has been caring for Jessie the last couple days. It radiated from Jud's laughter as he played with his cousin, Ella, this evening. Grace came from my parents, who drove several hours from vacation to be with us, and my mom, who later cleaned our house (and boy did it need it!). Grace flowed in the tears of others who identified with us in our pain today. Furthermore, it flooded us in e-mails, phone calls, visits, and prayers from people all over the nation, many who don't even know us.

God's grace is all around us. I want eyes to see.

Ironically, one of the greatest graces came after Jud had been given an oral sedative before the MRI (he had been struggling and crying so much to that point), and though drug-induced, we got to experience his joyful smiles for a few moments in a sea of fear and pain. Grace.

I want eyes to see.

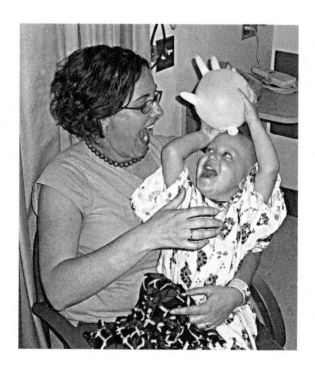

Journal Entry: Saturday, June 16

The Mingling

It is amazing how easily joy and pain can mingle together.

As we await a meeting with the pediatric neurologist to discuss Judson's progressing condition, we have tried to find some semblance of normalcy in our lives. It has been a challenge as we continue to see a decline in Jud's abilities. However, today we decided to go to the pool. We thought Jud might enjoy a little buoyancy in the water, and we figured it's about time for Jessie to have her first experience taking a dip in the waters that regularly beckon to us through the window in their bedroom.

It was great! We had a fabulous time. Jessie was her usual, easygoing self and had no qualms about being in the cool water. Jud was a little hesitant at first, but once in the Jacuzzi, he came alive! He smiled from ear to ear almost the whole time we were in the spa. He seemed to enjoy his independence, which he has recently been losing, as he stood on the side of the Jacuzzi by himself, splashing and laughing, splashing and laughing, and splashing and laughing some more. It was wonderful!

In fact, I think the pain made the joy just a little bit sweeter.

Letter 3: Monday, June 18

Dear family and friends,

We have hope.

As you know, we had an appointment with the pediatric neurologist this morning. It turns out there have been two issues at play.

The first issue has to do with the significant decline we have observed over the last couple weeks in Jud's ability to perceive things in front of him, balance, etc.—a symptom called ataxia. Of all the horrible things that can cause this symptom, it turns out the neurologist believes it is the most innocuous of them all; an autoimmune response in Jud's system attacked his cerebellum, probably due to some type of virus (don't worry, it's not contagious!). This was the best possible scenario we could have expected. The amazing news is that the doctor expects the brain will begin to compensate, and we should soon begin to observe these symptoms improving, even over the next two weeks. Amazingly, no treatment should be necessary!

The second issue is something that was unexpectedly discovered from the MRI. It appears there is some ventricular damage in Jud's brain, apparently affecting his mobility. The doctor believes this occurred when I was pregnant with him, possibly from my preterm labor at thirty-one weeks of pregnancy with Jud—he may not have gotten enough oxygen in-utero (full-term is forty weeks). The symptoms are currently most visible in the dexterity of his ankles. Fortunately, the doctor is hopeful that, with treatment, Jud can regain full motion (although we're told he may never be an Olympian). Local surgery on the affected parts of his body may be required, or at the very least, time in a cast and therapy. In two weeks, when we meet again with the neurologist, we'll find out more about the course of action.

We are so grateful! We have gone from fearing that Jud had a terminal illness to fearing that he would be disabled for the rest of his life to now hoping that he will have full function of his body again. Furthermore, we might not have discovered the ventricular problem in his brain if not for the symptoms of ataxia. The doctor indicated that it may be a long road to recovery and a lot of work, but that feels like *nothing* to us, compared to the alternatives we thought we were facing.

God has been so good to us during this time. The mobilization of his people on our behalf has been both amazing and humbling. We have had people all over the nation and even overseas praying for us. *Thank you!* This trial has reminded us how the Lord uses his people to be an instrument of his grace and love. We have been so blessed by your e-mails, calls, and visits.

As we come to mind, would you persist in your prayers for God to completely heal Jud's body? Please also pray for us to continue to have eyes to see how God wants to manifest his character through this process! Please pray that when things are particularly difficult or frustrating in the treatment process, we will keep our sights on the goodness and grace of God and maintain a posture of thankfulness.

We are so grateful to all of you for your love!

With much hope,
Christina (on behalf of Drake too)

Letter 4: Friday, June 22

Dear family and friends,

Thanks to all of you for being hopeful with us over the news we received about Jud's health from the pediatric neurologist on Monday. Unfortunately, we have found ourselves back in the whirlwind.

We had been told that we should expect to see improvements in Jud's symptoms right away, but on Tuesday, Jud showed significant signs of decline. It was *so* discouraging! We decided to call the neurologist for more answers, but our message went unreturned. On Wednesday, Jud's symptoms were just as bad, if not worse. We tried again to reach the neurologist, but to no avail. At this point, we began (somewhat frantically, I might add) exhausting every avenue we could think of to get Jud the care he needed, but nothing seemed to be panning out. Finally the neurologist returned our calls late Thursday afternoon and said we could bring Jud in to see him in the morning.

After observing Jud this morning, the neurologist was truly perplexed by his symptoms. It was immediately clear that his initial diagnosis was inaccurate. In the previous visit, he had not focused enough on Jud's inability to "see" or perceive things in certain lines of vision and seemed to have based his diagnosis more on Jud's walking difficulties. He admitted that everything was now "a big question mark" in his mind. He gave us an immediate referral to see a neuro-ophthalmologist.

We just returned home from our visit with the neuro-ophthalmologist. He was able to pinpoint one of Jud's symptoms as "convergence insufficiency." As we understand it, this means that each eye works fine independently but not in tandem. This is a neurological disorder, but the doctor could not identify the cause. The next step was to re-read the films from Jud's MRI, paying particular attention to the brain stem. The doctor could not yet give us a prognosis. It is possible there are other symptoms that still have yet to be identified. Furthermore, we do not know whether any of these issues could be tied to the ventricular brain damage that was discovered on the first reading of the MRI.

We are, once again, hanging in the balance, while longing to see our precious little boy fully functioning again. It breaks our hearts to see Jud lose so much of his independence; he needs to be carried (or he scoots or crawls) most of the time now, he cannot feed himself very well anymore, and he has a much harder time engaging with people because he cannot see. Yet we already observe him beginning to make compensations for his deficits. He is trying so hard to be "normal" (it is amazing how much of a self-image such a little guy can have).

Admittedly, I am at the lowest point I have been throughout this process. We are emotionally and physically drained and still have quite a mountain to climb. The ups and downs have worn us thin. And, quite frankly, everything has been pretty confusing as we try to understand Jud's condition while maneuvering through the health care system. We trust that God is working in these circumstances and surrender it all to him. We continue to covet your prayers for Jud's complete healing.

On a brighter note, Jud turns two and a half this weekend (we celebrate his half birthday on June 24th because he was born on Christmas Eve), and we are dedicating both Jud and Jessie at church on Sunday (this has been on the books for over six weeks). Therefore, we will be surrounded by family this weekend (both our biological and church families). What a gift!

Thank you all for your love and support!
Christina (on behalf of Drake too)

Journal Entry: Wednesday, June 27

Jud's Vision

A friend from church brought us dinner tonight. While we were eating, Jud had a sippy cup directly in front of him, less than a foot away on the table, and he asked us, "Where is my drink?" We helped him find it, along with the rest of his meal.

Jud's symptoms continue to decline. He has a hard time seeing much at all now (an issue of neurology, not eyes), which affects many of his abilities. This is the most prominent of his symptoms, but he also cannot walk well (severe stumbling and falling).

A few minutes after I helped Jud find his cup, Drake asked me how I was doing. I responded, "It's killing me, as I realize that this could be our reality."

Jud quickly piped in, "Don't say killing, Mommy."

Drake began to cry.

The pain of our circumstance is ever-present and raw; the emotion strikes us each at different times.

"Are you crying, Daddy?" Jud asked. "Why are you crying?"

"All the problems we have been having have been hard. We want you to be able to see and walk again," Drake responded.

In that moment, Jud began quoting, word for word, the story of Job from his toddler Bible[5]. "One day a man ran to Job. 'Your children and animals have died,' he said. Then Job got sores all over him."

Drake cried harder.

"Do you want me to hold you, Daddy?"

Drake replied, "That would be great, Jud, but why don't you finish eating first."

Jud continued with the story of Job. "Did Job get angry at God? No! 'God gave me all I had,' said Job. 'I will still love him.'"

Our emotions flowed.

Jud may now be almost blind, but in that moment, both Drake and I wanted Jud's vision: eyes that see God's grace with an unfluctuating faith, despite circumstances. We have so much to learn from our precious little man!

Letter 5: Friday, June 29

Dear friends and family,

I hope you will indulge me with another long e-mail; I am realizing that I find it somewhat cathartic to process through our circumstances by writing to all of you, so thank you for bearing with me.

It has been a tough week here at the Levasheff abode.

On Tuesday, Jud had an appointment with his ophthalmologist, the doctor who has been most amazing through this process. He said that the team of doctors working with Jud had basically ruled out every diagnosis we had received to date. After discussing everything with him, it became clear to us that the pediatric neurologist we have been working with is out of his realm of knowledge. Furthermore, he did not listen well to us and set us back an entire week with misdiagnoses, ignored calls, and sending us all over the map to see other doctors who were not relevant to the core issues. Very frustrating! (We're sorry to have taken you on this roller coaster with us!)

The next couple days were spent fighting the Kaiser health care system to get Jud's medical records released to us, obtain a referral to a new neurologist, and file grievances. I felt like I had the phone implanted in my ear.

Per several recommendations, we had the chief of Neurosurgery at CHOC (Children's Hospital of Orange County) take a look at Jud's MRI films. Based on his observations and Jud's symptoms, he said that the diagnoses we had been given were "ludicrous," and he was baffled that certain tests had not yet been performed. This confirmed our frustrations with Jud's current neurologist.

We were finally able to get a referral for Jud to see the chief of Neurology at Kaiser Sunset in Los Angeles this morning. She was fantastic! She listened very carefully to our concerns, asked for a complete developmental history, examined Jud thoroughly, and explained her observations from the MRI. Unfortunately, her conclusions were heartbreaking.

There is probable demyelination in the white matter of Jud's brain, which basically means that the messages to and from his brain to various parts of the body are flawed (confirmed also by the doctor at CHOC). In Jud's case, the doctor believes there are two possible causes: infection or genetics. Though not wanting to rule out the possibility of infection, the doctor did not think this was the most probable cause because the demyelination in Jud's brain was symmetrical, and in cases of infection, it is usually patchy and irregular. By process of elimination, this means that Jud's condition is likely the result of a genetic disorder that can "show up" anytime.

Until further testing is done, the doctor did not want to discuss any of the numerous genetic diseases that could potentially be causing this type of condition. However, most discouraging was the fact that few of these diseases have definitive treatments, and we may continue to see deterioration in Jud's abilities. Much is still unknown, but the probabilities are hard to swallow.

The new neurologist ordered lab work and another, more involved, MRI called a Spectroscopy, which will occur sometime next week. We also have an appointment on Monday, July 9, for a neurogenetics clinic that involves several different doctors who will collaboratively analyze Jud's symptoms and test results in an effort to make a definitive diagnosis.

The beauty in this situation is found in Jud. His mental abilities and personality have been unaltered, so we are relishing his laughter, singing, funny quips, and sweet demeanor.

Drake and I are struggling; it has been so hard to have the body of a fully normal-functioning boy rapidly deteriorate before our eyes. We want to remain faithful, faithful to the God who created and loves Jud. We want this situation to shape the very fabric of our family, individually and collectively, that God may be glorified. We want to trust in his goodness.

We ask that you continue to pray with us for complete healing of Jud's body. We do not presume to know what God intends in this situation, but we believe he is the Great Healer and trust that his good work will be accomplished. To that end, we surrender.

Having been on the other side, we realize it is sometimes hard to know what to say or do in this type of situation. Many of you have expressed a desire to help. Please keep praying for us when we come to mind. It also means so much to get your e-mail responses—it reminds us that we are not alone! Though we have not been/may not be able to respond to all your e-mails, they have meant more than you can imagine.

In his grip,
Christina (on behalf of Drake too)

Journal Entry: Wednesday, July 4

His Perfect Design

The diagnosis and prognosis for Jud's condition is currently concealed from us, but I find peace in knowing it is completely known to God; it is part of his perfect design.

Oh God,

You created Jud's inmost being;

You knit him together in my womb *(what a gift!)*.

I praise you because he is fearfully and wonderfully made *(whether healthy or sick)*;

I know that full well *(though it aches to see him sick)*.

His frame was not hidden from you when he was made in the secret place.

When he was woven together in the depths of the earth, your eyes saw his unformed body *(whether genetically whole or diseased)*.

All the days ordained for him were written in your book before one of them came to be *(each breath yesterday, today, and tomorrow is known to you)*.

Psalm 139:13–16 (personalized)

O Lord,

You have searched me and you know me *(I surrender to you)*.

You know when I sit and when I rise;

You perceive my thoughts from afar *(all the anxiety, pain, fear, confusion, frustration)*.

You discern my going out and my lying down;

You are familiar with all my ways *(my moments of sobbing, my efforts to escape the pain, my moments of numbness, and my moments of peace).*

Before a word is on my tongue, you know it completely, O Lord *(may it be praise!).*

You hem me in—behind and before *(security!)*;

You have laid your hand upon me *(I feel your grip).*

Such knowledge is too wonderful for me, too lofty for me to attain *(I cannot comprehend it, but I trust it!).*

Psalm 139:1–6 (personalized)

This has been a longtime favorite passage of mine (ever since I memorized these verses at Hume Lake Christian Camps when I was in sixth grade), but never before has it been so poignant.

Journal Entry: Thursday, July 5

Endure

Though we long to numb it, discard it, delete it, dismiss it, eliminate it, purge it, transfer it, or wipe it out, pain cannot be taken away or removed.

It must be endured and hopefully redeemed!

Letter 6: Saturday, July 7

Dear family and friends,

I know it may be hard to believe, but I am going to give you a *brief* update on Jud.

He had his second MRSpectroscopy yesterday in LA. It went far better than our last experience, which felt like God's merciful hand upon us.

We go back to Los Angeles on Monday for the neurogenetics clinic. A geneticist, metabolosist, pediatric neurologist, and possibly some other doctors will all review Jud's history, development, symptoms, and test results to try and ascertain a diagnosis for his condition. We are longing for answers but are also desperately afraid of what we might hear (many of the genetic disorders are ultimately fatal or result in a vegetative state). As you can imagine, our hearts are heavy. We ask that you join with us in prayer on Monday; please pray for our strength, for the doctors to have wisdom, and please continue to pray for God to heal Jud's body. Your prayers are dear to us!

Much love and gratitude,
Christina (on behalf of Drake too)

Journal Entry: Saturday, July 7

Quite a Contrast

An MRI takes images that measure contrast in the brain, but it was the contrast between Jud's two MRIs that is an image worth comparing.

Yesterday was Jud's second MRI, a Spectroscopy. Admittedly, Drake and I approached the event with dread. The first MRI incident, three weeks ago, had been so difficult that it was hard to imagine walking through the experience again.

The two occurrences were like night and day.

First and foremost, Jud had an amazing attitude! Last time, he cried and screamed during most of the preparatory events, which was completely understandable considering the circumstances. This time Jud was short on sleep (we had to wake him at 5:30 a.m. when he usually gets up at 8:00 a.m.) and he had not been able to eat or drink anything for over seven hours (last ate and drank at 6:00 a.m.—preparation for the MRI began at 1:00 p.m.), yet, through all the poking, prodding, measuring, and testing, Jud smiled and chatted with the nurses. He was our usual sweet and content little guy, displaying not even an ounce of fear or protest.

Secondly, we did not have to observe or assist the nurses in starting the IV line. Last time, the oral sedation had already started to wear off when, on the first attempt, they were unable to thread his vein. Meanwhile, we were holding Jud down as he flailed and screamed in pain. This time, though we wanted to be able to comfort him, it was actually a gift not to be there at the time they started the IV. They carried Jud away in a state of "loopy" happiness.

God was extremely merciful with us today!

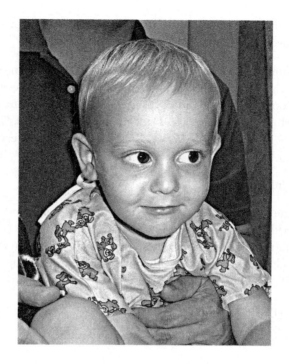

Journal Entry: Saturday, July 7

A Bellowing Voice

At the hospital yesterday we had some downtime in the waiting room prior to Jud's preparation for the MRSpectroscopy. Jud, being the social butterfly that he is, would ask, "What's your name?" when he sensed someone nearby. He also occupied himself with magazines by pretending they were books about turtles and fish; he is quite a storyteller and had the people around him in stitches.

But my favorite moment came when he declared, "Mommy, I want to pray for your balance."

"Oh, thank you, Jud, but I think my balance is okay. Why don't you ask God to heal your balance?" I replied.

He climbed up into a chair nearby (he still has the strength to climb), and with a bellowing voice for all in the waiting room to hear, he said, "Dear God, I just want to pray for Mommy's balance and Daddy and Aunt Danielle, Uncle Marty, cousin Ella, Cameron, Collin, Carson, and Avery Joy. Amen."

"Amen!" I echoed.

All the women in the room began gushing, oohing, and aahing with comments about how adorable and cute Jud is, and of course, I was proud; but more than that, I was reminded of why God adores children—the innocent hearts that approach his throne with anything and everything on their minds.

Lord, please help me lay it all at your feet.

Journal Entry: Sunday, July 8

Tree of Life

> Hope deferred makes the heart sick, but a longing fulfilled is a tree of life.
>
> *Proverbs* 13:12

We desperately desire for God to heal Jud! Yet I am afraid to hope. I am afraid to hope that God will actually restore our boy to health, because our hearts are already sick, and the delay of hope brings more brokenness.

However, we long for the faith that is able to see and experience God's supernatural healing hand. We want to reach out and touch the cloak of our Lord Jesus wherein he says, "Your faith has healed you" (Mark 5:24–34).

Faith and hope go hand in hand. How can we have the faith that he will heal if we don't actually hope for it?

Then the question remains, what if God's perfect plan for Jud does not include healing? How do faith and hope integrate with the omnipotent design of our Lord? It is said that "the prayer offered in faith will restore the one who is sick and the Lord will raise him up" (James 5:15, NASB). Is this a promise? But what about all the faithful, hopeful people before us who have prayed for God to heal, yet watched a loved one die? Hope deferred!

I grapple with these issues each moment of every day. I do not understand how faith, hope, and the sovereignty of our almighty God fuse together, but I surrender. I surrender to a God who loves me in the midst of my confusion, frustration, and pain. I trust him.

May I prove faithful, and may my longing lead me to the tree of life.

Sunday, July 8

A Father's Plea **by Drake Levasheff**

Ask and it will be given to you.

Matthew 7:7

So I'm asking, Father. And I'll keep asking. Please heal Judson!

I ask only by the blood of Jesus. Only through him do I come to you. Thank you for receiving me into your throne of grace.

I acknowledge that there is nothing I can do to deserve an answer to prayer. It's not dependent on whether I pray more or less. My right words won't make the difference. My right arguments won't mean much to you either. In short, Judson's healing is not on me. It's not in my hands.

You alone give life and breath. You were there when Judson was conceived. You knit his body together when he was hidden in the womb. You hold the power of life in your hands.

If you wish for Judson to be healed and whole, it will be done.

So I'm asking, Father. I only have a little faith. So I'm asking you to grow it into faith that moves mountains and plants trees in the sea. I'm desperate for that right now.

So I'm asking, Father, heal Judson! Only you can save him!

Your ways are mysterious. But your purpose in the world is evident; you are bringing together to yourself a redeemed people who declare your praise to all the nations—they (we) are blessed to be a blessing.

Judson is such a blessing. I hear his speech. I see how he treats people. He speaks kind, affectionate words in a world that hungers for love. I see the trajectory of his life (you alone are sovereign!), and I see good from him all his days for your people and the world you sent Jesus to save. By giving him long life with the use of all of his capacities, the blessing will be multiplied. While it pierces me as a father to think of losing my son, the thought of losing this beautiful soul to death or fruitless life pierces me doubly.

And so I have boldness to ask this of you.

What is more, I consider the current circumstances and the glory and praise that will reverberate to you at Judson's deliverance. Only you know how many people are praying for Judson's healing and restoration. From what little I know, Judson's life and health are on display to people all over the country. His healing will be a testimony to believers in the

West who need to be reminded that you heal today, and to many who do not know you, that you are alive.

And so I beg you, Father, heal Judson!

Until you do heal Jud, grant us grace that we may endure patiently, that you may be glorified!

Journal Entry: Sunday, July 8

Perspective

I am scared. I think I am more scared than I have ever been. Jud has his neurogenetics clinic tomorrow, and it feels like we could walk away tremendously relieved, still completely perplexed, or absolutely devastated.

Tomorrow feels like one of life's greatest pivot points.

Ironically, tomorrow won't change our circumstances, only our knowledge and understanding of our circumstances. Ultimately, it may shift our perspective, and our perspective governs our emotions.

But what is your perspective? I want my perspective to be your perspective, Lord; I want your perspective to penetrate my heart. Therein, I reflect on these truths:

> I am beloved of God.
>
> God will not give us more than we can handle.
>
> His mercies are new every morning.
>
> He knows the end from the beginning.
>
> His plan is perfect.
>
> He works all things together for good.

He is trustworthy.

O dear God, I surrender. I surrender all. In this and every circumstance, please shape my perspective as unto you.

Letter 7: Monday, July 9

Dear family and friends,

I know so many of you have been praying for us, particularly today, and we thank you.

Unfortunately, our worst fears are being realized.

From all the testing thus far, the geneticist and neurologist have every reason to believe that Judson has a leukodystrophy. Leukodystrophies are rare genetic diseases that affect the myelin sheath, the material that surrounds and protects nerve cells in the brain. Because damage to the sheath slows down or blocks messages between the brain and the rest of the body, the types of symptoms that Jud is having begin to appear, problems with movement and vision. There are no cures. Symptoms will gradually get worse over time, potentially affecting speech, hearing, and other capacities.

For some leukodystrophies, there are a couple treatments that sometimes help slow down the progression of symptoms: stem cell or bone marrow transplants. However, it is a genetic disorder that most often ends in a vegetative state and ultimately death (usually within six months to two years after symptoms appear, though some live ten years or more).

The doctors did a spinal tap (which was so hard to see Jud go through) and drew blood again for more tests. They want to ensure that everything else has been ruled out and provide a definitive diagnosis, narrowing it down to the actual leukodystrophy that is affecting Jud. The MRI and MRSpectroscopy tentatively point toward adrenoleukodystrophy (ALD), but there are over thirty different leukodystrophies, many of which could be possibilities; though I have never seen it, my understanding is that the movie *Lorenzo's Oil* is about a boy with ALD.

I have no words to describe what we are feeling. We are so broken!

Any healing of Jud's body would be an absolute supernatural miracle of God. We beg and plead, yet I am admittedly afraid to hope for such. What if God's omnipotent, almighty plan for our family does not include Jud's healing?

My friend reminded me today of a passage in the book of Mark where a father asked Jesus to heal his son:

> "If you can do anything, take pity on us and help us," he cried.
>
> "*If* you can?" said Jesus. "Everything is possible for him who believes."
>
> Immediately the boy's father exclaimed, "I do believe; help me overcome my unbelief!"
>
> *Mark* 9:14–29

I yield and surrender to the plan of our loving and gracious Lord but also cry out for him to help me overcome my unbelief!

Thank you for walking this journey with us. If we come to mind, please continue to hold us up with your prayers, and if you have the faith, please ask God to heal our precious boy!

In his merciful hands,
Christina (on behalf of Drake too)

Journal Entry: Monday, July 9

First Sucker

It took two nurses and Drake to hold Jud down and still for the spinal tap today; I just sat there after hearing horribly bleak news, weeping as I watched the clear fluid drip out of his back into the tubes for testing. From my vantage point, the pain was excruciating.

After they were finished, we sat Jud's sweaty little body upright, and the nurse gave him a sucker. His first sucker ever! It was as if all the trials of the moment suddenly vanished from his memory, and he was in heaven (and so were we as we observed his delight).

He clutched his sucker, giving it a little lick periodically for the next several hours—while waiting for some paper work, while his blood was being drawn, and on the ride home from Los Angeles. He even continued to clutch it while he fell asleep in the car.

Not only was the sucker sweet to him, it was sweet for us—a reminder that after intense pain often comes reward and delight. Oh, dear Lord, may it be so!

Tuesday, July 10

Letter **by Daniel Adelseck,**
Christina's brother

Dear family and friends of the Levasheffs,

Everything we have heard from the doctors and read concerning Judson's condition is clear. There is no human intervention or skill that can restore or completely halt the deterioration of his abilities. Even today we noticed signs of deterioration in his speech.

Many of you have asked how you can help. At this point, we have a tangible but challenging request for all of you. Consider praying with us that God would heal Jud, without doubting. "He who doubts is like a wave of the sea, blown and tossed by the wind. That man should not think he will receive anything from the Lord" (James 1:6–7). Moreover, please begin to pray earnestly. In Luke 18:1–7 and in Luke 11:5–13 we are taught that God responds to persistence and boldness.

Our chief aim is that our prayer would be according to God's will (1 John 5:13–15) and that we pursue it for God's glory and not our own selfish desires. If God chooses to heal Judson, it would be a tremendous testimony of his greatness and power. We would share in the great joy, but the glory would be his alone. Seek him humbly, but please do not be afraid to ask with us. He is our Father.

Please also consider fasting, that your heart and mind may be resolute in interceding for Judson. May it be a reminder that all of our sustenance and days belong to him alone. Please consider setting aside some time this week to join us in fasting, even if it is only a meal or two. May the hunger be an instrument to move us to fervent petition for Jud, as well as turning our hearts and minds toward him. Please also consider stopping whatever you are doing on Saturday evening at 7:00 p.m., and join us in corporate prayer, wherever you are, for Judson. Ask God to heal him. We would rejoice to see God prolong his life and restore his health. Thank you for your support. Drake and Christina remain moved by the outpouring of your love.

In Christ,
Daniel Adelseck (Christina's brother)

Letter 8: Tuesday, July 10

Dear family and friends,

We received a call from Jud's pediatric neurologist this evening. She had obtained the information from the spinal tap, which continues to confirm the diagnosis of a leukodystrophy; Jud's spinal tap shows no sign of a viral attack but rather shows high levels of a protein that is indicative of a leukodystrophy disease. The doctors are now trying to determine which leukodystrophy is ravaging Jud's body.

The elders of our church, along with other loved ones, gathered in our home this evening to pray for Jud. James 5:14–15 says, "Is any one of you sick? He should call the elders of the church to pray over him and anoint him with oil in the name of the Lord. And the prayer offered in faith will make the sick person well; the Lord will raise him up … "

We are so thankful for the community of believers, locally, across the nation, and overseas who are entreating the Lord for Jud's healing.

Science says that Judson's path has already been written, but we know our God is the Great Healer yesterday *and today*. We want to see the movement of his healing hand, that unto his name be glory!

I just finished reading J. P. Moreland's book *Kingdom Triangle*[6]. Amongst many other things, he talks about God's power and glory being displayed through healing. I was challenged and would encourage others to pick up this book.

With love and gratitude,
Christina (on behalf of Drake too)

Letter 9: Wednesday, July 11

Dear family and friends,

We are still waiting for some blood tests to confirm which leukodystrophy is attacking Jud's brain. We expect to hear back from the doctor on Monday. I had mentioned ALD previously, but that has not yet been confirmed—the blood test, which is essential to the diagnosis, is scheduled to be performed on Friday. We have received *many* e-mails about the various treatments to help abate symptoms for ALD— thank you for researching on our behalf. We are aware of the time-sensitive nature of some of these treatments and have spoken directly with one of the nation's leading doctors for leukodystrophies, who specializes in ALD. He has been and will continue to be a wonderful resource, whether or not Jud ends up being one of his patients. We have family members who have been on the phone and Internet consistently to ensure that Jud is getting the best possible care; rest assured that our son is in good hands.

Jud has never been much of a crier; he certainly whined and fussed, but he rarely cried. This is changing. We are seeing a progression of behavioral changes (we have read that this should be expected) that are currently appearing as frustration and crying. As this disease manifests itself in him, it is a constant struggle to know how to respond to his behavior.

We are constantly grappling with yielding expectations. It is heart-wrenching!

We are also seeing signs of a couple other symptoms creeping in. Though today was a little better than yesterday, Jud's speech seems to be becoming more garbled. Of all the symptoms, this will be, without question, the most heartbreaking for us. In so many ways, Jud has been defined by his ability to speak and articulate his sharp mind from such an early age—truly exceptional! (Though I am admittedly biased, I think many who know him well would echo these sentiments.) To see these capacities dissipate will tear us at the very core! O God, have mercy on us!

May the Lord grant us wisdom and patience as we seek to raise a child who honors him with his heart and choices, while also having his body impaired by a nasty disease!

With love and gratitude,
Christina (on behalf of Drake too)

Thursday, July 12

Praying with Confidence **by Drake Levasheff**

One of the issues that I have been wrestling with as we pray for Jud's healing is this question of what it means to pray with confidence. My experience has been that God hears prayers—especially the small, manageable kind. You know, things like work issues and job interviews, struggles with relationships and financial needs—things that can be answered through us or other people. But I don't have much experience with God answering prayers that he alone can answer. I've never seen him heal a boy in a situation like my son's. And even if I've heard about it, I've come to think of those cases as the exception, not the rule. My practical theology says this: There are certain things that only God can do, only he doesn't do them very often, so don't hold your breath.

For the past month or so, I've sensed a tension between this way of looking at God, prayer, and healing, and the passages in the New Testament on prayer and healing. They are straightforward and simplistic. "Ask and it will be given to you" (Matthew 7:7). "If you remain in me and my words remain in you, ask whatever you wish, and it will be given you" (John 15:7). "And the prayer offered in faith will make the sick person well; the Lord will raise him up..." (James 5:15). And there are many others. Suffice to say that it was the expectation of the early Christians that God would hear their prayers.

A lot of believers I talk to today are uncomfortable with letting these passages stand as they are. They talk about exceptions, or they make clarifying points like, "If this is God's will." I've been guilty of this too. But why do we do this?

To put it simply, those passages don't line up with our experience. We don't have our prayers answered. And so we doubt. And maybe we see someone we care about suffer or die even after we prayed for his or her healing. And we have to find a way to explain the tension between the passages and the lack of answered prayer—so we tiptoe around the passages. Or we simply say that whatever we asked for wasn't God's will because he is sovereign (which of course, he is!).

Could it be that we simply lack faith in God? I've seen plenty of people who love and obey God, love other people, know his Word and want to see his will done in the world, but when they ask, they do so without confidence, as if their request is an imposition. Or they're afraid that the request might not be precisely what God wants. I know I've been guilty of this. It reflects a lack of confidence in God and a passivity—there are things we know with certainty about God and his purpose in the world, but we don't act accordingly.

Let's talk more about Jud's situation now.

I take for granted that God is able to heal (even if this is a genetic issue, he is able to heal Jud). I also take for granted that he is compassionate and full of mercy. His heart is grieved to see Judson and the rest of us suffer through this—don't forget about the shortest verse in the Bible: "Jesus wept" (John 11:35). In light of these things and the afore-mentioned passages above, I think we can pray with confidence that God will hear us.

But many would ask how we can know that healing Judson is God's will. My first response is to say that it is God's will for us to ask—see the passages above and many others. When we fail to pray for something because we question whether it's God's will, we put our own doubts ahead of the Bible's clear instruction to make requests. So if we're concerned about Jud's life and we fail to pray for his healing, or we pray with doubt, then we're out of God's will.

My second response is that we need to learn to bring what we know about God to bear in the circumstances we face. In the current situation, a few thoughts come to mind:

- From what we know about God, we know that he has compassion for Jud and the rest of us who suffer through this. Even if he allows it, it grieves him to see it happen.

- If Judson is healed, this will bring God glory and praise among his people—no doubt, many will be encouraged.

- If Judson is healed, many unbelievers (including, but not limited to, our family and friends) will see what he has done and may be saved.

- If Judson is healed, it will serve as a testimony to everyone that God answers prayer and works supernaturally to heal. We in the West need to be reminded of this!

- ° We know that such an answer would have a pivotal effect in our family. We have believing relatives on both sides of the family, but while we love and know God and his Word, we're not characterized by a faith that expects God to dramatically intercede. This lack of faith for supernatural intervention would only be reinforced if God does not heal Jud.

- ° We believe that healing would also make a difference in the church. Our interactions with the community of believers have given us the impression that while some believe God will heal, others seem to believe that Jud's deterioration and death is just a foregone conclusion. We want to see the faith of our brothers and sisters increase.

- ° Death for Judson would rob God's church and world of a blessing. (Don't just brush this off because his dad is saying this!) He's a kind and affectionate boy who already has a knack for encouraging others—and until recently, has been very articulate. In a world in need of encouragement, I believe that he will be a fruitful tree who could produce a hundredfold. It would grieve me to see that influence lost.

I do not presume to know everything—God's ways are certainly higher than mine! But the above scripture and observations give me a basis to pray for Jud with confidence. I'm really starting to believe that God is going to heal our son.

Please join me in humble, persistent, confident prayer, for the Lord bids us to pray in such a way!

Month Two:
Crying Out in Affliction

Letter 10: Friday, July 13

Dear family and friends,

We continue to feel *so* supported and lifted up by people. We weep (in a good way) as we read your thoughts, prayers, encouragement, and kind words. I still have yet to respond to a single e-mail, or send a thank you, or return a phone call, and I realize now that I might continue to have difficulty doing so because the outpouring of love we have received has been so huge.

Though impersonal, may I express my gratitude here? From flowers delivered to our home, gifts left at our door, visits from unexpected friends, incredible meals made by loving hands, cards in the mail, touching phone messages, the hiring of a housecleaner, gifts for Jud, offers for babysitting, offers for vacation, financial assistance, donations of sick time to Drake from the Vanguard University community, and the list goes on and on, we are so touched!

Thank you, most importantly, for your prayers. Thank you for petitioning God regularly for Jud's health to be restored. Quite frankly, though it is strange to say in this context, I have never felt as loved as I do now by people and especially by God.

A couple that we don't even know came over last night to encourage us, pray with us, and pray over Judson. Their son was miraculously restored to complete health by God several years ago (it is a neat story), so they know the power of our healing Lord. We were blessed by their testimony and encouraged by their faith-filled prayers for Jud!

With love and gratitude,
Christina (on behalf of Drake too)

Journal Entry: Friday, July 13

Day by Day

Each morning I wake up, take a deep breath, and remind myself that the mercies of our Lord are new each day. And then I imagine what it would be like to walk into Jud and Jessie's room and have Jud jump out of bed, venture across the room, and be able to look me directly in the eyes again as he expresses his usual excitement about some toy he had in his "big boy" bed with him.

This has not yet happened, but I believe in a God wherein it would be his great pleasure to see his glory manifested this way.

However, my hope is not in the miracle of healing (though I pray it be so!); my hope is found in a loving Father who asks me to place all my burdens at his feet. My hope is found in the fact that Jud's body will one day be made whole again, whether it be here on earth or in the loving embrace of his Maker. My hope is in his promise to walk alongside me and renew me day by day.

When I begin considering what our lives may be like in weeks or months or years, I cannot bear it; I am overcome with grief, fear, anxiety, and hurt to the point where my body is writhing and retching in pain. That is when I am reminded that none of us knows what tomorrow will look like; therefore, we must live for today.

I have been given the strength for today.

I can bear up under my circumstances when I do not worry about tomorrow. In fact, I can delight in today. I have much to be thankful for: an amazing, faithful, honorable, and gifted husband; supportive and loving family; gracious and encouraging friends; and I am part of the family of God that is blessing us daily with generosity, kindness, and prayers. I also have been gifted with two beautiful children whose laughter, singing, and smiles are music to my senses.

O that I may maintain a posture of gratitude and not worry about tomorrow, for tomorrow will take care of itself.

Letter 11 : Saturday, July 14

Dear family and friends,

As stated previously, we are very thankful to be in direct contact with one of the nation's leading doctors for leukodystrophies. My dad spoke with him this morning to discuss Lorenzo's oil and determine whether or not it would be fitting for us to start using it to treat Jud even though we are not yet certain that his leukodystrophy is ALD. The doctor informed us that Lorenzo's oil would not be beneficial for Jud, even if he has ALD, as his condition has already progressed too far.

We did, however, send him all Jud's medical records that we have received, along with his MRI films. The doctor will evaluate the information to determine if there are other potential treatment options to affect the progression of symptoms.

Thank you for continuing to think of us and pray for our beloved boy!

Much love,
Christina (on behalf of Drake too)

Journal Entry: Saturday, July 14

Engage It

Toward the end of May (as I was starting to notice Jud stumbling more but didn't think much of it), we had an end-of-the-year banquet for our women's Bible study at church. A woman shared about her life journey and particularly about her trials related to her husband's severe, chronic, post-polio condition. There was a time of Q&A at the end, and I had raised my hand to ask a question, but we ran out of time before it could be answered. And so I was left still wondering, "What is the best way for people to walk alongside you in your pain? What touches you most?"

My greatest challenge when I know someone is struggling has been not knowing what to say or do; I admittedly keep a safe but "loving" distance because I feel powerless, inadequate, and uncertain as to how I should engage the pain (and maybe even a bit afraid to engage it). Anything and everything I do or say seems insufficient. At times it is even awkward, and I bumble through, probably saying silly things, being too silent, maybe not being silent enough, but basically feeling incompetent. This is likely because I unconsciously or even consciously want to remove the pain. This is my tendency. Thank goodness so many people are gifted with mercy and compassion.

Nobody wants to walk through pain alone. In my current circumstance, I am absolutely moved and sometimes even shocked by the tears, sadness, and grief of others, many who don't even know Drake and me or little Jud. I am realizing that pain is pain. We all have had hurt in our lives (this is the reality of a fallen world). We all know what it feels like to ache. We can relate, at least on some level. To walk alongside people in their pain requires us to engage a little bit of our own pain. It may hurt, and it may be messy, but this is love!

And so my question is being answered.

Rather than try to remove the pain (which is actually impossible), engage it, even if it hurts to do so. I have been extremely humbled to be a recipient of such love and compassion, and I am learning. In my present circumstance, I am learning what it means to truly walk alongside people who hurt. It is being modeled to me. People have engaged my/our pain in a way I never could have dreamed or imagined. They have allowed themselves to hurt with us in order to love us well. There could be no greater gift!

Many are teaching me. I want to internalize it in hopes that I too can be a tool of mercy and compassion for others, just as many have been for me.

Journal Entry: Saturday, July 14

Have Mercy

Drake and I have wondered what aspect of a leukodystrophy actually leads to death. So, in search of some answers, I went exploring on the Internet today. (I know what you're thinking: "Don't do that!") I read stories of kids who have lost their life to this disease. I was overcome with fear and pain. This is such an insidious, vicious, horrifying disease as it slowly sucks every bit of bodily life from its victim. Their bodies become stiff, even to the point of being unable to smile, they can no longer swallow and therefore need a feeding tube but ultimately die from being unable to breathe.

I cannot bear it. I cannot bear to see my precious little boy walk this path. I cannot bear it!

I have already watched this affliction destroy Jud's mobility and vision. It is currently attacking his speech, while we are also seeing glimpses of dysphagia (the inability to swallow). Moreover, this disease affects behavior; Jud is far more irritable, and the disease is staking claim on his impulse control too. The pain is excruciating, not just for him, but for us. It hurts. It hurts so much!

The deterioration has been so rapid! It was just two months ago that Jud was playing at the park outside our home—looking for roly-polys (pill bugs), slipping down the slides, climbing the ladders, and socializing with the other children who crossed his path. Now he has no interest in the park that is just feet away from our front door.

Oh, dear God, I beg you to have mercy on Jud!

Please heal his body here on earth. Please allow him to run and jump and slide again. Please change the very structure of his chromosomes, that they may be whole. Please remyelinate his brain. Please restore all his bodily functions to full capacity. Oh Father, please have mercy on Judson! To you be all glory.

In the meantime, be still my soul.

Letter 12: Sunday, July 15

Dear family and friends,

Our church prayed collectively for Jud and our family today. What a blessing!

Since this is a genetic disease, many people have been wondering about Jessie. We still need to determine what type of leukodystrophy is destroying Judson's body, and then we will have a better idea as to whether or not Jessie is at risk. Some leukodystrophies just affect males, whereas others attack both genders equally. Once we have more detailed information regarding Judson, testing will be done on Jessie's blood to get some of these questions answered.

Fortunately, we have a peace, along with high hopes, that Jessie is unaffected and does not have the same genetic disorder. However, we would covet your prayers for her as well.

Thank you all for your concerns about our precious little girl too!

With love and gratitude,
Christina (on behalf of Drake too)

Journal Entry: Sunday, July 15

Surreal Versus Real

This is all still so surreal. It is surreal to believe that my son is fighting a terminal and incurable disease. Though we see his symptoms, it doesn't seem possible that Judson's life is slipping through our fingers. Pain like this has only grazed us before—could it really have fallen square in our laps? Never in a million years could I have imagined that we could face losing Jud at such a young age, especially to a genetic disease. How "random" is that!

Well, we know that it is not random. We know that God not only foreknew what we would be experiencing in July 2007, but he actually hand-selected Jud and our family before he was even born (and even before we were born) to allow us to walk this path for his name's sake. It is crushing and humbling all at once. We want to be faithful in this tumultuous call he has for us.

Our church family prayed for us today. What a gift! And as I stood there, holding Jud on stage and glancing out at the faces before me, I also knew that God had hand-selected this community to walk this path with us. We have only been part of our church for exactly one year (we began attending in July of 2006 right after we moved to Costa Mesa), but they are proving to be incredibly faithful brothers and sisters to us, beyond what we could have ever dreamed. Many do not even know us personally, but they are pouring out their love upon us.

We also have our former church community in Fullerton that has been regularly lifting us up in prayer, writing words of encouragement, and taking our needs before the church body. We have the Vanguard University community surrounding us. We have many from our former Biola community caring for our needs. We have people from our church families during childhood lifting us up. We have people across the nation and overseas who do not even know us who have chosen to fast and pray on our behalf. This is the family of God at work! It is incredible and overwhelming to be recipients of this kind of love. This is the gospel, God's love poured out to people. I cannot imagine walking through life, much less this path, without our brothers and sisters of faith.

This situation with Jud may still be surreal, but the love we are experiencing is very real.

Journal Entry: Monday, July 16

Questions

By nature, I am a very inquisitive person. I want answers, and I'm often not afraid to ask.

In our present circumstance with Jud, many have wondered if I am tempted to ask, *Why?* Sure! I want to understand how God is specifically using and plans to use this situation (yet it should be noted that I am already seeing his hand at work). But I believe the truest answer to the question, *Why?* has been displayed throughout Scripture—God wants to and will manifest his glory through every circumstance. In this lifetime, we may never actually know the exact reason why God has chosen for us to walk this path (though I hope we see glimpses), but we are confident that the Lord of the universe, our Father, will display his glory through this situation.

A more appropriate question may be, *Why not?* Why shouldn't the God of all creation choose this for Jud and our family? The temptation is to feel that I am entitled to a life that looks a certain way or is pain free. I am not. No one is.

I think the most critical question for me to be asking is, *How?* How do I live well in these circumstances? How do I learn to recognize that each breath, whether mine or Jud's or anyone else that I love, is a gift? How do I deal appropriately with the pain? How do I allow the truth of God's Word to shape my experience? How do I pray in this situation?

I expect my mind will continue to race with questions as it tries to reason through the pain of the circumstance, but it is my hope that the questions I am asking lead me down the path of deeper understanding to the one who calls me beloved.

Tuesday, July 17

Letter **by Drake Levasheff**

Dear family and friends,

In the next couple of weeks, I'm planning to do a preliminary study of the Gospels to find out what they teach on prayer and healing (I'm hoping that this will direct my prayers and increase my confidence as I pray for Jud). As I do, I'll be looking at Jesus' teaching on prayer and healing, the prayers that he prays, and his healing miracles. I invite you to study the Scriptures along with me to see what they teach in these areas.

Yesterday I read through and reflected on Mark's Gospel. As I read, a few things stood out to me.

First, it was evident that Jesus' healing miracles give us a window into God's compassion. On more than one occasion (for example, Mark 1:32–34), Jesus spent hours healing the sick and casting out demons. Because of his healings, the crowds pressed in all the more—and many who touched him or his clothing were healed (Mark 6:54–56). As the crowds pressed in on him, he embodied the compassion of the kingdom with numerous healings. And at the same time, while Mark shares about the life of Jesus, he teaches us that God has compassion on the afflicted and is willing to heal them.

When I read about these healing miracles, I was struck by the assertiveness and often pleading of recipients of healing miracles and their friends and family. A leper falls to his knees and beseeches Jesus to heal him (Mark 1:40). In one case, four men tear into the roof of a house to get their friend healed by Jesus (Mark 2:3). Jairus, a synagogue leader, falls to Jesus' feet and implores him earnestly to heal his daughter (Mark 5:22–23). One woman pushes through a multitude just to touch Jesus so that she would be healed of a constant flow of blood (Mark 5:25–28). A Gentile woman falls at his feet and keeps asking that he would deliver her daughter from demon possession—she will not be refused (Mark 7:25–26; while this is not specifically a healing miracle, the author clearly considers this account to be in the same vein as those miracles)! Several people in Decapolis implore Jesus to heal a deaf and nearly mute man (Mark 7:32). Others in Bethsaida implore him to heal a blind man (Mark 8:22). Finally, blind Bartimaeus entreats Jesus to heal him, and after the crowd tries to silence him, he cries out all the more (Mark 10:46–48). By and large, they plead with abandon, and they plead until their requests are heard because they believe that Jesus can heal; if necessary, they will make a scene!

At the same time, Mark intends to teach us about faith, prayer, and healing; that if a request is made in faith, it will be heard. Thus, Jesus responds with forgiveness and healing to the faith of men who tear open a roof so that their friend can be touched by him (Mark 2:5). He tells a woman healed by touching his cloak that her faith had made her well (Mark 5:34). Jesus exhorts Jairus not to be afraid, but only believe that his daughter will be healed (Mark 5:36). Only once do we encounter a situation where Jesus' healing powers are inhibited—and that is because of the lack of faith they have in his hometown, Nazareth (Mark 6:1–6). A final miracle, the exorcism of a boy, provides evidence that anything is possible to the one who believes and at the same time emphasizes the importance of prayer (Mark 9:14–29).

If the healing and deliverance miracles in Mark illustrate the necessity of faith for answered prayer, the story of Jesus' curse of the fig tree and his subsequent teaching drives the point home. On a walk between Bethany and Jerusalem the week he was crucified, Jesus curses a fruitless fig tree, for he was hungry (Mark 11:12–14). On their trip back into the city the next morning, the disciples notice that the very tree that Jesus cursed had withered. When Peter mentions what happened, Jesus proceeds to teach them about prayer, exhorting them to have faith (Mark 11:22). Faith, Jesus says, trusts that God will give us whatever we ask and acts as though what has been requested has already been delivered by God (Mark 11:23–24). Such faith must be coupled with forgiveness (Mark 11:25).

My brief survey of Mark's teaching on prayer, faith, and healing revealed three significant points:

- Jesus' healings provide a window into God's compassion for the afflicted; he is willing to heal them.

- Those who petition Jesus for healing in the stories do so with abandon. They plead persistently and shamelessly for Jesus to heal.

- God answers the prayers of those who ask in faith, who believe that they have already received what they have asked for.

Such teaching encourages me to pray with even greater boldness for Jud's healing, for I know that God cares deeply for the afflicted. It teaches me to make my request assertively and persistently, even shamelessly. Finally, Jesus' teaching on faith encourages me to walk in the hope that if I've asked for Jud's healing, I can expect that God will give me my request when I ask.

With faith and love,
Drake

Letter 13: Tuesday, July 17

Dear family and friends,

We were touched by the community at Vanguard University today. They had a prayer meeting for us. It was a meaningful time, and we were certainly moved by the tears, prayers, and petitions on behalf of our family and Jud. We are so blessed that Drake's employment at Vanguard has allowed us to be part of this community of people.

We received some unexpected, inconclusive information from the doctors today, so now we must wait until all the comprehensive blood work is completed to hopefully provide a definitive diagnosis. Everything still seems to point to a leukodystrophy, but more information is necessary. We have had someone in the medical field describe neurology as an art as much as it is a science. It appears that Jud's case is not very cut and dry. The waiting for more information is hard, but the most difficult part is seeing Jud struggle. We continue to beseech God for healing, and we are so moved by the number of people doing so with us!

Much love and gratitude,
Christina (on behalf of Drake too)

Letter 14: Wednesday, July 18

Dear family and friends,

We just received word that they have discovered the enzyme that is likely causing Jud's leukodystrophy. Jud is deficient in *galactocerebrosidase* (GALC), which is indicative of Krabbe disease. All four of us are going to LA tomorrow to have our blood drawn for DNA testing. The doctor made it clear that this was not a definitive diagnosis until the DNA results are back, but it appears this mystery is gaining clarity.

Even though we knew that news like this was coming, it is still staggering and hit us hard. Furthermore, this disease is common among siblings, even females, so Jessie is definitely at risk, a possibility that would be absolutely devastating!

As with all leukodystrophies, Krabbe disease is fatal. We are, in fact, fortunate that Jud has lived this long. The average age of death for a child with Krabbe disease is thirteen months old.

We continue to covet your prayers in this trying time. We know that God heals and God hears. Our eyes are on him.

Love,
Christina and Drake

Journal Entry: Wednesday, July 18

Intricate Design

After we received a call from the doctor today informing us that Jud has a galactocerebrosidase deficiency, I began to read about the importance of this enzyme and other enzymes in the body. I was in awe.

There are more than three thousand known enzymes in the human body. They are the body's life force—involved in every human function. Vitamins, minerals, and hormones must have enzymes to work properly.

Galactocerebrosidase is just one little enzyme in the body, and yet a deficiency can lead to loss of everyday bodily functions and result in death. Just one little enzyme! Yet each of us has over three thousand of them, and for the vast majority of us they are functioning properly. This is incredible!

I had to pause for a moment and consider the amazing, intricate design of our bodies.

Could this kind of order and design spring from disorder and chaos? Impossible! It points to a magnificent, omnipotent Creator who is the giver of life. It is a wonder that any of us can take a breath, walk, sing, smile, laugh, eat, or cry!

So as I lay my head down to sleep tonight, I consider with amazement the one who gives life and breath and also yield my heart to him who can take it away.

Letter 15: Saturday, July 21

Dear family and friends,

The last couple days have been tough as the reality of our situation is sinking in, things are settling down, and we continue to see deterioration in Jud's body.

Having our blood drawn on Thursday went fine—it was just a long drive for something that took so little time. We must, however, note that Jessie was *amazing*. She didn't make even one peep or shed a single tear when they drew her blood. This is a perfect example of how much of a trooper she is. What a gift!

We are constantly amazed by the people who are praying for us and for Jud's healing—it feels like the numbers are growing exponentially every day. Thank you for letting others know about our precious son; this is such a blessing to us! Please continue to pray for God to restore Jud's chromosomes to wholeness so that our little boy might regain all of his abilities, and may God be glorified all the more through such a miraculous manifestation of his power!

I will say this again, and probably continue to say it—we are so touched and moved by your words to us. You would probably be surprised how often we check to see if anyone has written, though I apologize that we have responded to so few; it is one of the greatest ways God is encouraging us and holding us up during this time. I often wonder how lonely this journey would be if not for the technology that is allowing us to be in touch with so many so easily. We can't thank you enough!

Much love,
Christina (on behalf of Drake too)

Journal Entry: Saturday, July 21

Waiting

I feel like I am just waiting. I feel like I am either waiting for God to heal Jud or, as awful as it sounds, waiting for my son to die. In the waiting, I am having a hard time living.

My days are getting harder and harder as Jud becomes more and more needy, while becoming less and less capable. Furthermore, his ability to cope with life is diminishing, leading to much greater irritability. He bawls uncontrollably at any given moment, he is frequently frustrated, and in the middle of the night and during naps, he cries out with bloodcurdling screams that wrench my soul.

Furthermore, Judson doesn't want to be left alone anymore, even for a moment. When he is eating at the table, he asks us to hold his hand. When we are driving in the car, he begs us to touch him. When it is time to sleep, he pleads with us, "Will you lay with me?" We also regularly hear, "Will you sit with me? Will you help me walk? Will you play with me?" These are all endearing moments, but sadly, I feel physically and emotionally taxed much of the time. Yet I cannot possibly deny the requests of our dying boy!

I want to relish each moment with our little Jud, and there are still many wonderful moments of smiles and laughter, but these moments are fracturing my heart.

I am broken. I need more strength. I lack patience. I sometimes feel guilty. I need wisdom. I don't want regrets.

Oh, dear God, please help me. I want to live in the waiting, but today I felt like I was dying.

Journal Entry: Sunday, July 22

Treatment

It has been said that prayer for healing is like providing treatment for the sick. You do not give treatment just once; you treat the sick over and over until they are healed.

There is no treatment for Jud other than prayer!

This has become my constant prayer, my treatment, for Jud:

> Oh Lord,
>
> Your kingdom come
>
> Your will be done
>
> In Jud's body here on earth
>
> As it is in heaven.
>
> *Matthew* 6:10

Let the resurrection power of God's mighty kingdom, a place free of sin and death, with strength that gives life and breath, rain down upon Judson. May God's good, holy, and perfect will that despises affliction and pain eradicate this disease that is ravaging Jud's body and bring healing here on earth, just as it would be in heaven. Please engage your supernatural might today, dear Lord!

The enemy has come to kill, steal, and destroy, but Jesus came to thwart his work. Jesus' ministry as he walked among us provides a picture of God's power and compassion. Most importantly, he brought spiritual healing, but he also frequently freed people from physical afflictions as evidence of the presence of his kingdom. Jesus is the same yesterday, today, and forever. Therefore, we entreat him to pour out his kingdom in Jud's life and in our lives here on earth as a testimony to his resurrection power! Again, I pray,

Oh Lord,

Your kingdom come

Your will be done

In Jud's body here on earth

As it is in heaven.

Matthew 6:10

Journal Entry: Monday, July 23

New Every Morning

I shed numerous tears yesterday. On several occasions throughout the day, Jud consoled me by stating, "You're going to be okay, Mommy!"

Each time I heard these words they soothed and touched my soul like nothing else.

In the afternoon we were sitting together on the couch. As I attempted to put Jud's shoes on him—which is much harder now that his legs, feet, and ankles are stiffening—I just couldn't hold back the tears. This time, rather than telling me it was going to be okay, Jud began to sing.

"The steadfast love of the Lord never ceases. His mercies never come to an end ... "

I chimed in with him, "They are new every morning, new every morning. Great is Thy faithfulness, O Lord. Great is Thy faithfulness."[7]

And in fact, God's mercies were very new to me this morning.

Letter 16: Tuesday, July 24

Dear family and friends,

As I have stated previously, we have been in contact with one of the foremost doctors for leukodystrophies. After the discovery that Jud has a *galactocerebrosidase* deficiency, this doctor referred us to another doctor in Philadelphia, at Jefferson University, who specializes in this type of leukodystrophy. I e-mailed him yesterday, and this was his response.

> Dear Mrs. Levasheff,
>
> My lab was the one that actually did the testing for Krabbe disease on Judson's blood and found the low *galactocerebrosidase* (GALC) activity. That makes the diagnosis of Krabbe disease definitive. DNA testing will not add much to the diagnosis and is not needed for confirmation. We now have blood from you, your husband, and your daughter. This week, we will test all of you. We hope your daughter has GALC activity in the unaffected range. We already know one of the mutations in Judson's GALC gene, and we are still testing for another mutation. We should have results back to your doctor before the end of the week.
>
> Sincerely yours,
> Dr. David Wenger

This gives us definitive confirmation that Jud has Krabbe disease (which really didn't feel like new news to us), but we were amazed to discover we are in direct contact with the doctor that actually tested Jud's blood. How incredible is that?

Please continue to pray with us that Jessie does not have this horrible disease too. We cannot even bear the thought!

We will say it again. Science may tell us that Jud's course has been determined and that there is no hope, but we have hope in a living God who is as active today as he was when Jesus walked the earth. In our Western culture, we may not experience his supernatural power very often, but we pray with confidence, knowing he can move in miraculous ways!

With love and gratitude,
Christina (on behalf of Drake too)

Journal Entry: Tuesday, July 24

Two Mortals

Krabbe disease is an autosomal recessive disorder, meaning that both Drake and I are carriers of the disease. However, neither of us can point to anyone in our known ancestral history that had any type of neurological disorder. Nonetheless, it is still likely that this extremely rare recessive trait has passed down both our family lines for several generations, only to make an appearance when our two stories became one.

From the day I met Drake, I had an inclination that he was the man with whom I would be spending the rest of my life. Though we were actually on dates with other people that fated day, we were definitely drawn to one another (sorry Amy and Dave!). I vividly remember us bantering back and forth, quoting the movie *The Princess Bride*, and thinking to myself, "Someday we are going to look back on this moment together and it will be the beginning of a long history."

Indeed!

Drake is my soul mate. I believe we were meant to be together. In fact, God has had his hand in our relationship all along, even months before we actually met, and he has his hand on us now.

In light of our current circumstances, I am reminded of some of the words Drake wrote and shared with me in front of our family and friends on our wedding day eleven and a half years ago. They could not be more apropos.

> If the past is a testimony of God's grace to us, then tomorrow we will watch in amazement. We stand as two mortals coming together by divine power. How can we fail if we bow humbly before him? We can't see all that's ahead— what sorrow or tragedy, what grief might come. No matter what, we have a Father who loves us, who knows what is best, and who will complete what he has started in us. Let us lay hold of that which he has laid hold of for us.

Amen. Amen.

Wow! I married an incredible man.

Letter 17: Wednesday, July 25

Dear family and friends,

We have fantastic news. Jessie does *not* have Krabbe disease!

Here is the e-mail we received.

> Dear Mrs. Levasheff,
>
> Just so you know as soon as possible, Jessie does *not* have Krabbe disease. She probably is a healthy carrier like you and your husband. I will send the results to your physician. Jud-

son's GALC value is very low, reconfirming the diagnosis of Krabbe disease.

Regards,
David Wenger

Thank you to all who have been praying for her health. Praise God!

With a grateful heart,
Christina (on behalf of Drake too)

Journal Entry: Wednesday, July 25

Life Spared

We found out today that a life in our family was spared of a horrible, deadly disease!

Jessie Lynn does not have Krabbe!

Before hearing word from the doctor about Jessie's status, we felt like our lives were on the brink of complete and utter desolation. The thought of seeing both our children afflicted was more than we could bear.

Jessie's name means, "God is gracious." Yes, indeed! She is certainly a recipient of his grace, and so are we. Jessie's life was preserved from Krabbe, and now she serves as a symbol of hope.

As Jud is losing capabilities, Jessie is developing new skills. She has been taking her first steps, mimicking many sounds, and developing her personality. We find her to be a complete joy! She is quite the little dynamo, but very little ruffles her feathers. She laughs frequently, cries very infrequently, and smiles at everybody.

Life is very difficult right now, but we have hope. Jessie is a symbol of hope, and we have hope in a God of love and compassion. We picture the day when God rains down his miraculous power and releases Jud from this affliction wherein he regains all his capabilities—once again running to his sister and looking her in the eye as he declares his love for her.

Today we celebrate life—life spared!

Journal Entry: Thursday, July 26

Crabby Krabbe

When I first saw the word Krabbe, I thought it was pronounced "crab." We have since come to discover that this daunting disease is pronounced "crab-bay." Unfortunately, that hasn't seemed to change the fact that it makes Jud very crabby.

One of the initial and long-term symptoms of a child with Krabbe disease is extreme irritability. As horrid as some of the other symptoms are, this is currently causing me the most emotional hardship. Jud's behavior has changed dramatically over the last month or two, and we are at a total loss as to what expectations we can/should have of him.

A couple days ago, a woman from Drake's work brought us dinner. In an effort to introduce Jud and have him show his gratitude, I picked him up off the floor where he was playing to help focus his attention on our guest. He threw an all out tantrum—yelling, screaming, and flailing. I was absolutely mortified and at a total loss as to how I should respond. The woman was very gracious and talked about his behavior being typical of a two-year-old, but I was broken inside, knowing that this was completely uncharacteristic of our little man.

I grieve the fact that it is in these circumstances and because of these circumstances that so many people are meeting Jud for the first time, a time when he is not fully himself. Though some of his current behavior may be typical of two-year-olds, it was generally atypical for Jud. I want people to meet our sweet, tender, thoughtful Judson, not impeded by Krabbe.

I am torn apart, saddened, frustrated, embarrassed, and feel anxious when Jud acts out and it hits me at the very core of some of my greatest personal neurosis, including my pride and selfishness. I'm afraid of people thinking we've raised an unruly, undisciplined child. I tend to feel like Jud's behavior at this age is a reflection of our parenting, and my ego wants to be stroked, not smashed. Unfortunately, this is an issue that goes far deeper for me than Crabby Krabbe.

I am weak.

As my life currently spins out of control with the affliction of Krabbe, may his strength be made perfect in me.

Friday, July 27

Letter **by Danielle Jones**, *Drake's Sister*

Dear family and friends of the Levasheffs,

My name is Danielle Jones, and I am Jud's aunt, Drake's sister. I am writing because I have become aware of a need. It is hard for Drake and Christina to ask, so I am asking. As Jud's condition advances, it is becoming increasingly difficult for Christina to care for Jud and Jessie on her own while Drake is at work.

Many people have graciously offered to babysit, which is a wonderful gift. Yet, in talking with Drake and Christy, they have expressed that the greatest way to meet the need for them right now would be to hire someone to come alongside Christina and help care for the kids at home. There are a few reasons for this. First, this would allow Christina to continue to have a sense of "normalcy" like being able to go about her usual activities like moms' group, grocery store, etc., which is impossible when multiple people are coming in and out each day. Second, this would allow Christina time with the kids, to take advantage of the moments with sweet Jud and be able to provide consistency for Jessie too. Additionally, if our sovereign Lord chooses not to heal Jud, he will continue to deteriorate and will require increased and more skilled care; it is imperative to Drake and Christy that he be cared for in their home, which may require large, out-of-pocket expenses.

So many of you have asked the question, "How can we help?" At this point, it appears as though they will not be incurring large medical treatment bills, so one gift that we can give Drake and Christina is the assurance that they will be able to care for Jud well in their own home. A fund has been established in Judson's name at their church.

Thank you for walking through this with us,
Danielle Jones (Drake's sister)

P.S. I was talking with Drake, and he said something that really touched me. He said that if Jesus were here on earth today and we saw him and asked him to heal our boy, what would we say? Would we say, "Please, if it is in your will, would you heal him?" No. We would not ask in this way! If Jesus were here, walking among us, we would run to him, and we would plead with him, "Please, Jesus, please heal our boy."

Journal Entry: Friday, July 27

Perfect Gift

Back in 1998, I was diagnosed with a disorder that affects fertility. Because a majority of women with this disorder require some type of fertility treatment to get pregnant, Drake and I began to assume that without intervention we would remain childless. Time passed, and Drake was busy working on his PhD at UCLA, and I was enjoying my work as an administrator/instructor at Whittier College, a local, private institution.

Imagine our surprise and utter shock when, after more than eight years of marriage, we discovered I was pregnant. Incredible! We were being given the gift of life.

Here are some snippets from my journal at the time:

> April 22, 2004: In my heart of hearts, I really did not believe that I could get pregnant. Is the test accurate? Am I reading it wrong? I've stared at it for several minutes in disbelief. Me? Pregnant? Are my eyes betraying me? As impossible and unreal as it seems, the proof is staring me in the face. I am pregnant. Father, I believe you have placed this baby in my womb—I stand in awe and trust that your timing is perfect. Wow! We are now vulnerable to new pains and even the loss of this child. Please help us to give of ourselves freely despite the fear of pain. I feel so weak and frail. Thank you for loving me.

> April 25, 2004: Father, I feel ill-equipped for parenthood. Please prepare my heart, mind, and soul for this person you have entrusted to our care. I stand in awe that you are knitting someone together in my womb!

May 6, 2004: Lord, please keep me from anxiety and worry over the development of "Little Levy." I find myself fearful and protective of this life inside me. I long for this baby to thrive, not just survive. Will you guard this child? I already love "Little Levy" immensely! I also pray you continue to shape my heart and open my arms to you in surrender as I am given the opportunity to care for this precious person.

May 25, 2004: Dear God, I am so thankful for the chance to have a person developing in my body. What a gift! What a blessing! What a miracle!

After being pregnant for thirteen weeks, we had a huge scare. The doctor actually told us that we had miscarried. But we begged him for an ultrasound to confirm. Lo and behold, they found our sweet little baby moving around with a perfect heartbeat. Praise God! Our little gift was alive!

At nineteen weeks, I experienced complications with my fibroids, which lead, once again, to concern for our baby's health. After a few trips to the hospital, the fears subsided, and we continued to have a healthy pregnancy.

At thirty-one weeks, I went into full-blown, pre-term labor. I was contracting every minute (with extreme pain due to back labor) and beginning to dilate. They injected steroids and other drugs in preparation for the early arrival of our child. However, after several days of hospitalization and numerous medications, the doctors were able to stop contractions. I was put on bed rest, and amazingly, the precious life that had made its home in my womb actually settled in for a full-term pregnancy.

Judson Drake Levasheff was born on Christmas Eve 2004, and on Christmas Day, we brought home the greatest gift: life!

When someone crafts us a special gift, do we say to the giver, "Why did you make it this way?" Of course not! We are just grateful.

Our precious Jud has been and remains a tremendous, unexpected, and perfect gift!

Letter 18: Friday, July 27

Dear family and friends,

When we received the news that Jessie does not have Krabbe disease, I screamed it to all in the house and then started to weep. How wonderful! Her little life has been spared of this affliction. Thanks be to God!

Sadly, seeing as we are still in a sea of grief and despair with Jud's condition, the rejoicing did not last as long as it might have under other circumstances. Thank you for rejoicing with us, and may we ask that you even rejoice *for* us, because this truly is reason for much praise!

Judson woke this morning in such good spirits. It is amazing how much this impacts our thoughts and feelings during each day. He is an absolute pleasure!

We are being so blessed and touched by people—so many who don't even know us. One such example came in the mail a couple days ago. Both Drake and I received beautiful, hand-made prayer shawls from a church in Missouri that heard about our situation—my friend Sarah told her mom, Carla, who told her sister, Stella, who told her sister-in-law, Robyn, who told her church. A woman in the church, Sylvia, made our shawls. Wow! I cannot begin to express how this blessed us! FYI, I take mine to bed with me now.

Many of you have mentioned the Make-a-Wish Foundation to us. We have, in fact, applied for Jud. We will let you know what comes of it.

We continue to be amazed that God put us in direct contact with the doctor who has been testing Jud's blood (and Jessie's too). We have yet to hear back from Jud's actual doctor, the geneticist in Los Angeles. If not for Dr. Wenger's e-mail responses, we would still be waiting for a confirmed diagnosis and not yet know that Jessie does not have Krabbe. Talk about an unexpected blessing!

Much love,
Christina (on behalf of Drake too)

Sunday, July 29

The Kingdom, Healings, and Jesus' Prayer
by Drake Levasheff

And he sent [the twelve] out to preach the kingdom of God and to heal the sick.

Luke 9:2

He welcomed [the crowds] and spoke to them about the kingdom of God, and healed those who needed healing.

Luke 9:11

Heal the sick who are there and tell them, "The kingdom of God is near you."

Luke 10:8–9

Your kingdom come!

Luke 11:2

As we pray for Judson, we've wrestled with the way in which we approach the throne of grace. One of the main questions that arises is whether we can know God's will with regard to Jud. On the one hand, we know that we ought to ask, even with confidence. On the other hand, we wonder why we should expect God to heal Judson when we know of so few situations in which God has miraculously healed in our day and age.

In the midst of my study and writing on Luke (yes, I'm still working on it), I began to recognize a connection between the Lord's prayer (Luke 11:1) and some passages on the kingdom of God and healing that really have me thinking. As I read Luke 9 and 10 (which includes the first three selections above), I see a strong relationship between the proclamation of the kingdom and the healings performed by Jesus and his earliest followers. In a very real sense, the healings serve as evidence of the presence of the kingdom of God. Through the healings, Jesus and his followers proclaim the presence of heaven's power and heaven's compassion on earth.

When they were not proclaiming and demonstrating the presence of the kingdom, Jesus taught his disciples to ask for it. So they prayed to the Father, "Your kingdom come!" (Luke 11:2) Or, as Matthew says, "Your kingdom come, your will be done" (Matthew 6:10). Either way, they were seeking God's kingdom and God's will. They were pleading for him to reign on earth the same way he does in heaven, where righteousness reigns and the afflicted are healed. Because healings demonstrate God's reign, one should expect that answered prayer for God's kingdom to come should involve healing.

As I apply these passages to the circumstance we face with Jud, I begin to get greater clarity about God's will. If Luke is to be believed, healings demonstrate and proclaim the presence of the kingdom of God. When we ask for God's will to be done and his kingdom to come, healing is bound up in his will, for healing demonstrates the presence of his kingdom. So as I pray for Judson, I don't know how I pray for God's kingdom to come and his will to be done in this situation without expecting that God will stretch forth his hand to heal. This sort of thing seems to be in Luke's thought, and so it will be in mine as well!

Journal Entry: Sunday, July 29

Dance

> Life isn't about waiting for the storm to pass;
> it's about learning to dance in the rain.

Anonymous

I saw this quote on a website I visited today, and it gave me pause to consider. Though I desperately want this hurricane to pass, how might we waltz in the downpour?

Today Jud rode a carousel at the mall with a grin that went from ear to ear. We danced. It was wonderful!

Monday, July 30

Letter **by Drake Levasheff**

Dear family and friends,

Before I say anything else, let me tell you how much your support, assistance, and prayers have meant to us! God has enabled us to stand in this trying season because you have stood with us.

You have been walking with us, so you know how insidious Krabbe disease is. Our experience of Jud's deterioration and research on the disease have confirmed that his healing is beyond the reach of medicine; humanly speaking, he is marked for a heartbreaking death, which we should expect within months to years. Because we believe deliverance from this affliction is within the Lord's reach—and his alone—your faith-filled prayers mean a great deal to us (James 5:13–18).

This Saturday, members of our family and friends will be praying and fasting as a means of drawing near to God and entreating him to heal Jud. We believe that God hears the prayers of his people—and all the more as we draw near through fasting.

So I'm inviting you to join us in forgoing one or more meals on Saturday and instead spend that time before the throne of grace. Please also consider stopping what you are doing Saturday sometime between 8:00 and 9:00 p.m. to pray for Judson's healing. (We'll have people at our house praying for him during that time.)

If God lays it on your heart to pray and fast on Saturday, would you let us know? Knowing all those who are praying for Jud will increase our faith as we pray.

With gratitude and hope,
Drake (on behalf of Christina too)

Journal Entry: Monday, July 30

Affliction

To spend any time with Jud is to clearly see that he is afflicted both physically and emotionally.

Not only can Jud no longer walk on his own, he cannot stand and rarely crawls anymore. He uses his arms to scoot around but is most content to sit in one place, lie down, or be carried. His body is stiffening, and fatigue is ever present. His vision is almost completely gone as well. He would certainly be considered legally blind now, for it is very infrequent that he sees much of anything. Instead, he uses his sense of touch to try and "see" the world around him, and even, much like a baby, has started putting things in his mouth again, "tasting" his world. His voice has been losing strength, quality, and clarity. He talks much more quietly as he tries harder to articulate words that used to flow off his tongue with ease. The skin around his mouth is slightly chaffed due to excessive drool as swallowing gets more difficult. It is not uncommon for him to choke while eating, and he also appears to be losing his appetite a little bit. Fortunately, his mind is still very sharp.

All of these physical afflictions lead to emotional affliction as well: frustration, anger, irritability, discouragement, and even sadness. There is now a seriousness to Jud's countenance that is hard to see in such a young child.

All this to say it is absolutely heartbreaking for anyone who watches Jud struggle. Even for the hardest of hearts, it would be impossible not to have intense compassion for him.

How much greater must God's compassion for Jud be—a two-and-a-half-year-old child in anguish, whom he made in his image and deeply loves. In fact, his love and compassion for Judson runs even deeper and greater than that of Drake and me, his earthly parents; this is enough to guarantee that God is concerned about our son's sickness.

Krabbe disease, and every other sickness, is a result of the fall of man, and though God permits such affliction, he can overrule sickness to his own glory. Therefore, the very nature of sickness means we must ask God to thwart the work of the enemy.

It is certainly not always God's will to heal the sick, as we often see; but I am beginning to believe that it often is his blessed will.[8] We see again and again in the Bible how Jesus healed the sick, and in those cases where it was not God's will to heal, he made his reasons known. Will he not also do the same for us?

I humble and surrender my heart to the only one who can release Jud from this affliction.

Letter 19: Tuesday, July 31

Dear family and friends,

Though Jud is clearly struggling, we also have been having many moments of humor, laughter, smiles, excitement, and fun, for which we are extremely grateful.

Thank you for continuing to uphold us in prayer,
Christina (on behalf of Drake too)

Journal Entry: Tuesday, July 31

Risk

> Faith is believing what we do not see, and the reward for this kind of faith is to see what we believe.
>
> *Saint Augustine*[9]

> Indeed, there is nothing God will not do for those who will dare to step out in faith onto what appears to be only a mist. As they take their first step, they will find a rock beneath their feet.
>
> *F.B. Meyer*[10]

I have been so challenged by Drake's faith during our current circumstances. He has inclined his ear to the Lord both through study of the Word, prayer, and quiet listening. Upon hearing God, he has truly stepped out in the mist, believing God will miraculously heal Jud. I believe this is a kind of faith given by our Lord.

> Faith is a gift of God. The Holy Spirit gives faith. Faith is not an emotion, but it is simply a resting upon the revealed will of God, whether that will of God is revealed in his Word, or by revelation from the Spirit. When God's Word has a plain promise to us, it would be sin not to believe that promise and risk God.
>
> *John R. Rice*[11]

Drake is risking God. He is sharing his faith for Jud's healing, not concerned about saving face, despite the unbelief of so many (believers and unbelievers alike). Willpower does not create faith; God gives faith, and God has given Drake faith, faith for Jud's deliverance from Krabbe disease. And "where God gives the faith, God does the healing. Where God is not pleased to heal in a particular case, he will not give faith for healing" (John R. Rice[12]).

I too want to be attentive to the Lord's voice. And as God is giving me the same faith, I want to step out with Drake and risk God. Therein, may we find a rock beneath our feet and the reward of seeing what we believe.

Journal Entry: Wednesday, August 1

Dry and Clean

Prior to the onset of Krabbe disease, we had been potty training Jud. He had a potty chart, and with the accumulation of smiley faces, he would earn various special potty toys: a ground FX Matchbox car, a monster truck, and even Thomas the Tank Engine. We would also give him "dry and clean" chocolates, when he was able to stay "dry and clean."

However, as we began to see a decline in his abilities and the whirlwind of health concerns began, we decided to stop potty training. We ceased asking Jud if he needed to go potty, no longer talked about the benefits of the potty, and stopped encouraging him in that direction.

Well, Jud had a different plan. He was determined to earn Thomas and the other "potty" toys. Out of the blue one day, a couple weeks ago, Jud declared that he needed to use the potty. Though hesitant at first because it used to take thirty to forty-five minutes before we would see any action, we decided to oblige him. Sure enough, he went immediately. Then he did it again and again until we started to realize that he was potty training himself. A couple nights ago, he even stayed "dry and clean" the entire night!

Jud has shown such determination, a characteristic that is

especially encouraging during this season. At a time when so much of his body is out of control, it has been a joy to see him take pride in controlling his ability to use the potty!

Journal Entry: Thursday, August 2

French Fry

Jud currently needs to be carried from place to place in the house. I usually pick him up and carry him on my hip, just like I do with Jessie. However, a couple days ago we were tackling and playing, and I decided to throw him over my shoulder in a "fireman's carry." As I playfully patted his bum, I said, "You're my sack of potatoes."

Jud quickly quipped, "No, I'm not. I'm a french fry!"

I just laughed and laughed, amazed by his sense of humor. Jud laughed too!

I later asked Drake and my mom if either of them had taught him that, and they both said no.

Where he comes up with these things, I don't know, but he certainly has great comedic timing!

Friday, August 3

Healing and the Kingdom of God
by Drake Levasheff

> Now Simon's mother-in-law was suffering from a high fever, and they asked Jesus to help her. So he bent over and rebuked the fever, and it left her. She got up at once and began to wait on them.
>
> *Luke 4:38–39*

I've long taken for granted that sickness and even serious illness are simply the way of the world. They're a permanent part of our experience, and so I've grown to accept it. Even when we began to realize that Judson's condition was very serious, perhaps life threatening, I still thought of it as one of those things that just happens.

As I've read the Scriptures, prayed, and reflected, my perspective has changed dramatically. I recall that God created our bodies perfect, but sickness and decay came into the world because of the fall and the work of the serpent. The earth became the devil's dominion with its kingdoms under his sway (Luke 4:6); sickness and disease are not simply accidents but an expression of his malevolent rule. When we see how Krabbe disease is destroying Jud's body, it's not at all difficult to believe that the enemy has a hand in it; this sort of deterioration wasn't part of God's intention when he created the human body.

Luke's Gospel acknowledges as much about sickness and disease. The devil rules the kingdoms of this world (Luke 4:6)—and sickness, demon-possession, and grief are part and parcel with his rule. But Jesus' ministry proclaims something different: the nearness of God's kingdom in compassionate healings and exorcisms, in powerful preaching and teaching (Luke 9:2, 11; 10:8–9). He supplants Satan's kingdom and replaces it with his rule, where mercy and righteousness reign.

Jesus' first recorded healing in Luke—of Simon's mother-in-law (above)—reinforces this perspective on healing. Jesus does not simply pray for Simon's mother-in-law or put his hands on her; rather, he rebukes the fever. He does not accept sickness as the way of the world but treats it like a foe to be defeated. This was central to his kingdom proclamation and ministry; Jesus sought to supplant the malevolent kingdom of this world and replace it with God's kingdom, where righteousness and compassion reign. He enlisted his followers to partner with him in the work (Luke 9:2; 10:8–9).

What does this mean for Jud's situation? Judson's illness is not a neutral thing that just happens but the fruit of Satan's work that began in the Garden of Eden. It is our call to continue Christ's work by standing against the work of the enemy and ushering in the rule of God. In Jud's case, that means interceding on his behalf to see this heinous disease removed from his body, that he be fully restored. If Jesus were here, it is what he would do, and we are called to continue his work (John 14:12).

As I incline my ears to the Lord, I am convinced that God intends to defeat the enemy and deliver Judson from this heinous disease. What is more, I believe that the Lord intends to plunder Satan's kingdom by redeeming many lost souls. Join us in praying in faith to that end!

Letter 20: Saturday, August 4

Dear family and friends,

God has mobilized his people, and *many* are pleading with him for Jud's healing. Just as it is for us, let it be an encouragement to you. Well over a hundred people are fasting today, around twenty people will be in our home tonight praying and worshiping collectively, several hundred are praying today and will also be praying sometime between 8:00 and 9:00 tonight (PST), and thousands have been praying throughout the last two months. May this spur you on to pray with boldness and confidence today, for you are not alone! God works mightily when his people on earth agree on anything.

> I tell you the truth, anyone who has faith in me will do what I have been doing. He will do even greater things than these, because I am going to the Father. And I will do whatever you ask in my name, so that the Son may bring glory to the Father.
>
> *John* 14:12–13

With much love and expectancy,
Christina & Drake

Letter 21: Sunday, August 5

Dear family and friends,

What an incredible day we had yesterday! The Spirit of God

was certainly present in our home. We gathered with friends and family for an evening of praise, worship, confession, reading of the Word, and prayer. We were absolutely moved by what people shared and prayed, and while our hearts and voices called out to our Lord from below, Jud slept peacefully in his room above us. As people felt lead, they intermittently went up to touch him and pray over him, and remarkably, his rest was more quiet and calm than we have experienced in quite some time!

Many others were also present with us last night, though they were not in our home, but rather they were praying across the globe. We are completely humbled by the fact that numerous people are being mindful in prayer for our little boy. Thank you!

We are also absolutely confident that God not only hears our prayers, but his hand is moved by the faithfulness of his people, particularly when so many beseech him in agreement for one thing. We continue to pray with boldness, confidence, and expectancy and are blessed to have so many of you praying alongside us.

I have said it before and will say it again here: our hope is not in a miracle. Our hope is in the living God, the giver and sustainer of life, a Father of mercy and compassion who richly lavishes his love on us and offers his merciful hand to us each and every day. The very nature of who he is means we *must* bow before him and plead with him to deliver our precious Jud from this affliction. We are called to such!

As we incline our ears to God and submerse ourselves in the Word, Drake and I pray with more and more faith, believing that God wants to deliver Jud from Krabbe disease here on earth, as it would be in heaven, as a proclamation of his kingdom, that he may be glorified all the more. We constantly entreat him for full and complete restoration of Judson's body and submit our wills that they may be conformed to his.

As I have stated before, the greatest challenge is in the day-to-day watching Jud struggle. This is where we become weary, and our hearts grow sad. But this is also where your prayers have truly carried us!

We are so thankful that our dear friend, Sarah Hegenbart, has offered to join us in our daily challenges—to be an extra set of hands and to be a consistent presence in our home and particularly in Jud's life. We ask that you pray for her as well. May God give her physical and emotional strength well beyond what she can imagine.

God is good. May our lives be a testimony to that end!

Much love and thankfulness,
Christina (and Drake too)

Journal Entry: Sunday, August 5

From Loneliness to Community

Our church service this morning entailed open sharing, giving people the opportunity to express gratitude for the ways God has been working in their lives; it proved to be a powerful testimony of how the Lord moves through challenges to bring believers into community with one another. It reminded me of a short book I read titled *From Brokenness to Community*.[13]

Back in the middle of May (before our crisis with Jud's health), Drake took the kids so I could have an entire "day off." I spent about six hours at Crystal Cove beach reading, writing, praying, reflecting, and simply being still in the beauty of creation. Much of what I was pondering at the time had to do with the concept of community because I had been feeling lonely.

Here are a few of my reflections on the subject from that day.

> Community requires that one can be themselves, even in wounds and pain, and still be loved and accepted, that they don't have to conform to any preconceived notion of how they should be. In community, we grow together to become more fully ourselves. It moves us toward wholeness. We all have fears of being devalued and pushed aside, yet in true community we are embraced in our vulnerability and helplessness; we can be raw before others. Moreover, celebration must be at the heart of community, and celebration, even (and especially) in the midst of our brokenness, is rooted in giving thanks.

We do not choose our brothers and sisters in community; they are bestowed upon us (we may choose to be part of a particular community, but once we are a part, the people are given). A year ago we chose to be part of Grace Fellowship Church—the brothers and sisters we have been given are truly a gift! As with all communities, many are wounded and hurting, but I have observed and experienced that people are willing to enter into one another's pain for the sake of growth, that everyone may be cared for. I have found it to be a church in which people feel responsible for one another, where the weak are honored and there is a place for each person in their uniqueness.

Today our community celebrated by giving thanks for the ways God has been faithful. People gave glimpses into who they really are by being vulnerable and open; some expressed love and gratitude for one another, others praised God for his constancy, and many shared heartaches. But at the core,

I sensed that we simply rejoiced in being together, a broken yet redeemed people. At the heart of the celebration was a surrender to God Almighty, who brought us together.

I am so grateful to be part of the Grace Fellowship community, and upon choosing this community, I see that I have also been chosen for this community. I recognize that being a part of this or any other vibrant and blessed church requires more than just showing up and going through the motions. It is a call to enter in, to love, and to embrace my brothers and sisters in the same way that I long to be and have been loved in my brokenness.

And it is through my brokenness that I realize I have begun moving from loneliness to community.

Journal Entry: Monday, August 6

Joined on this Path

There are certain people with whom you cross paths, and the quality of their character and life is immediately apparent and enticing. Sarah is one such person for me. I met her back in 1998 while I worked at Biola University. Through my job, we had a year of consistent interaction that allowed us to develop a meaningful relationship. Since that time there have been changes in circumstances and proximity that have taken our friendship through seasons that have varied our opportunities to connect. This week we entered a new season.

Sarah, this longtime friend, has chosen to engage our current circumstances as a daily caregiver for Jud, coming alongside to help me from 8 a.m. - 2 p.m. on weekdays. She has not entered our home as someone detached from the situation, but rather as a one who knows and loves Jud and our family.

Herein lies a tremendous emotional engagement that reaches far beyond just a physical encounter with our son each day.

Today there was an instant when I looked into her eyes and saw the intense compassion she was feeling for Jud and then the apparent pain that ensued. Few words were exchanged in that moment, but I gained a whole new level of respect for my dear friend. I was struck by the reality of the sacrifice she is making to walk this path with us; she is choosing to put herself in a considerably painful circumstance. I'm not sure I've ever done it or could do it—engage the depths of someone else's suffering so significantly wherein it becomes part of the fabric of your own journey.

I am so thankful that our paths crossed and developed into a friendship ten years ago, and I am blessed to now have her join me on this path with Jud each day.

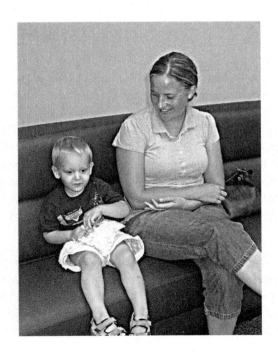

Letter 22: Tuesday, August 7

Dear family and friends,

We had a meeting with Jud's neurologist and geneticist in Los Angeles this morning (without Jud) to go over the final results of all the blood work for the family, further discuss his condition, and consider the options for care that are available.

The new blood work reconfirmed that Jud has Krabbe disease and also revealed that Drake and I are, indeed, carriers of Krabbe based on our enzyme levels. They were able to ascertain my gene mutation, but Drake's DNA mutation remains a mystery. Furthermore, based on Jessie's enzyme levels, it is probable she is a carrier too. However, this cannot be confirmed with absolute certainty because she does not have my gene mutation, so they must assume that she has Drake's "mystery mutation."

To give you an idea of how rare this disease is, one in approximately one hundred thousand to two hundred thousand people get Krabbe disease, and of those who are afflicted, less than 10 percent have Judson's form of Krabbe: type two. This makes the odds about one in every couple million. We already knew Jud was a "one in a million" kid, but I guess this makes him even more special! The challenge with this type of obscure disease is that there is very little research available for his form of Krabbe, and doctors have limited answers.

Our dialogue with the doctors about care for Jud was difficult. Per the doctors' recommendation, Jud will be put on hospice care immediately. This is very hard to swallow, seeing as hospice is for "end of life" care. We will know more once hospice contacts us in the next few days.

As much as none of the information we discussed today came as a surprise to us, it was a tearful drive home as the weight and gravity of this experience is settling upon us. Just two and a half months ago we had two healthy, normal-functioning kids, and in just a short time, our world has been completely turned upside down. We knew this day with the doctors had to come, and despite the difficult realizations, we continue to have faith and hope in the Lord Almighty. He is our Shepherd who is taking steps alongside us, comforting us in this very dark valley.

As stated in our last letter, we are extremely blessed to have our friend, Sarah, joining us in our day-to-day journey. We were touched yesterday when she shared about the online research she has done to try and understand Krabbe disease so she can lend the best support as she cares for/plays with Jud. She researched ideas and activities for blind children, physical and therapeutic exercises, and appropriate toys for kids with similar conditions. She knew far more than us! Furthermore, Jud is absolutely thrilled with her company. She offers tremendous patience and tender care. We feel so fortunate Sarah is willing to enter into this difficult circumstance with us, and we are especially thankful to all who have contributed to the Judson Levasheff fund to make this happen. You have no idea what a gift you are giving us!

As you can imagine, our emotions ebb and flow. Today has been a day of grieving, though even in the grief we have peace. We know God's plans, no matter how difficult the process, are good.

We continue to be amazed at the number of people who have heard our story and reached out to us. We often wonder who we are that so many have chosen to be attentive to our family and care about our trials when there are *so* many hurting and afflicted people. We wish there was more we could do than simply express our gratitude, but for now, please receive our simple thank you!

Much love,
Christina (on behalf of Drake too)

Journal Entry: Tuesday, August 7

A Welcome Disruption

I feel like my heart is breaking into a million pieces. Not only was it a difficult day facing some realizations after a visit to Jud's doctors, but I came home to a little boy whose very countenance grips me at the core.

It is actual physical pain I feel in my chest when I watch him struggle with things that we used to take for granted as commonplace. Today, due to his blindness, Jud couldn't put a puzzle together that at one time had become "too easy." Even while holding on to me, he couldn't stand up for me to get his shorts on him. He got frustrated because he couldn't find his dump truck that was just an inch in front of him. He was afraid to sit on the kitchen counter with me while I pre-pared food because he lacks the balance to keep from falling. I observed a change in his posture as he sat to play with "Alfie" the excavator. And his eyes were often half-mast as I gazed upon his handsome face.

Today I observed him through a lens of grief, and I could not bear the heartache.

This evening I lay there in bed with him and didn't want to let go of his frail frame. I felt his stiff ankles and longed for the touch of my hand to soften them. I massaged his calves as they spasmed and wished I had the power to ease his pain. I kissed his eyes, desiring for the softness of my lips to restore his sight. I listened to his voice as he struggled to express himself and then kissed his lips, hoping it would breathe life back into his speech. I stroked the hair on his head, entreat-ing God to heal his brain.

I finally tore myself away from the extended embrace of his diseased body and sat on the beanbag chair next to his bed. Without a word, he reached his fragile hand around the bed rail for me to hold. As tears rushed down my face in the quietness of his room, I started to tickle the palm of his hand. The silence of the night was interrupted with laughter. It was a welcome disruption from my pain.

Jud's body is broken, and my heart is broken. Please God, restore them both!

Journal Entry: Wednesday, August 8

Our Counting Game

"Mommy, I love you!"

"Thank you. I love you too, Jud."

"I love you three," my little guy responds.

"I love you four," I declare, seeing our game has begun.

"I love you five," Jud excitedly continues.

"No, I love you six."

"I love you seven, Mommy."

"I love you eight, Jud Bud."

"I love you nine."

"Oh, I like the number nine, but I love you ten!" I exclaim.

"Well, I love you eleven, Mama."

"I love you twelve!"

"No, I love *you* twelve!" Jud states emphatically.

"You like the number twelve, don't you, sweet man? What about thirteen?"

"Nope. I love you twelve!" Jud replies.

"Well, I love you more than anyone could ever count, Buddy Boo! You're a super loved boy!" I say with a deep sigh that communicates far more than the words that were just spoken.

Letter 23: Thursday, August 9

Dear family and friends,

We had our first visit from a hospice nurse today, and it continues to feel surreal that this is the path we are on. She basically did an intake and filled out numerous forms. The forms were too much for me to handle: Do Not Resuscitate, Mortuary Plans, and End of Life Care—that's simply *not* where we're at right now! That being said, it will be nice to have someone consistently look in on him each week, check his condition, and answer our questions.

Judson is starting to have difficulty using his hands. He hasn't been able to pick up his cup as easily (asks me to hold it *for* him), and he complained this evening, with great frustration, that his "hands are tired." I cannot begin to communicate with words how each instance of labored living pierces me. It feels like the life is being sucked out of his body ever so slowly, and we have to watch each excruciating moment as he experiences it. Our days are getting rougher and rougher, and all I can do is cling to Almighty God, my Father.

We continue to entreat God to move miraculously in his body. We had a timely call from a friend at church who is walking in faith with us. His comment was, "Let's just go for it! Let's do it! Let's pray fervently for God to move to heal Jud. No matter what the outcome, we will not regret having done so!" His words spoke to me and were a great encouragement; I hope they are for you as well.

Much love,
Christina (on behalf of Drake too)

Thursday, August 9

Jesus' Ministry, God's Compassion, and Healing **by Drake Levasheff**

Luke's telling of the gospel begins Jesus' ministry with a narrative about his visit to the synagogue in Galilee. The passage, which is without parallel in any other canonical gospel, serves to contextualize Jesus' deeds and ministry in the chapters ahead. Its location in the narrative means that it is critical to Luke's understanding of the Lord Jesus.

Jesus enters the synagogue in his hometown on the Sabbath. He stands to read and receives the Isaiah scroll:

> The Spirit of the Lord is on me, because he has anointed me to preach good news to the poor. He has sent me to proclaim freedom for the prisoners and recovery of sight for the blind, to release the oppressed, to proclaim the year of the Lord's favor.
>
> *Luke 4:18–19*

Jesus concludes by saying, "Today this Scripture has been fulfilled in your hearing" (Luke 4:21).

Luke means to show us that at the center of Jesus' ministry is compassion for the poor, afflicted, and oppressed. His Spirit-empowered ministry declares a new era of good news to them and brings healing and deliverance. Recovery of sight to the blind is emblematic of all healing ministry. The oppressed speaks of those dominated by the devil, and he enacted their deliverance. Jesus' ministry to the infirmed and captives reflects genuine compassion for them; he never turned any of them away.

But Jesus never sought his own purposes; he always pleased the Father and did his will. So when we watch Jesus' compassion for the sick, afflicted, and oppressed, we observe God's deep care and concern for them. God loves the poor, infirmed, and suffering, and so Jesus ministered to them. He touched them, he delivered them, and he healed them to demonstrate God's compassion. God is not distant from human suffering; he came so near so as to be affected by it.

When I look at Jud and see the heinous disease he is suffering, I am comforted to know that God has great compassion on him—even more than I do. And he is more than able to deliver Jud. With that knowledge, I will go to God tirelessly and shamelessly—like the persistent widow (Luke 18:1–8) and countless other petitioners in Luke. In this lies my hope and my calling today, for he bids me come.

Journal Entry: Thursday, August 9

Mickey Mouse

Sarah took Jud to Disneyland yesterday morning. She has an annual pass, and Jud is still young enough to be free, so she offered to be our "guinea pig" to discover whether or not Jud would truly enjoy "The Happiest Place on Earth" (before we consider investing in passes). This is the story of their morning, as told to me by Sarah.

When they first arrived, she took Jud straight to City Hall, where he received a Guest Assistance Card enabling them front of line privileges, etc. After that, seeing as Jud is such a vehicle connoisseur, she thought Autopia might be fun for him to drive the cars. Unfortunately, the ride was "too bumpy," so Sarah just held him 'til the drive was complete. Then they headed over to the new Nemo Submarine attraction. They were able to bypass the two-and-a-half-hour wait and get directly on the submarine, but unfortunately Jud got scared and started to cry, so he and Sarah disembarked before the adventure began (much to Sarah's chagrin since she's never experienced this new attraction due to the long lines). Seeing as the rides didn't seem to be "floating Jud's boat," Sarah opted for Toon Town, and this is where Jud found his stride.

There were various stationary vehicles for Jud to "ride," things to touch that made sounds, and he even went to Mickey's house for a visit. Jud grinned from ear to ear with Mickey, who took a lot of time with him; Jud played with his nose and touched his hair and asked about his eyes. He absolutely loved meeting the "real" Mickey Mouse!

Over his macaroni and cheese, applesauce, and chocolate chip cookie lunch (quite a treat!), Jud couldn't stop talking about Mickey. So on their way out, Sarah bought Jud a stuffed Mickey—the treat of all treats!

As they strolled to the car, Sarah could hear Jud talking but had a hard time hearing what he was saying, so when they got to the stoplight, she leaned down and asked him what he was doing. She heard him say, "I'm playing."

She responded, "Oh, you're playing?"

Jud, surprised that she didn't hear him correctly, emphasized, "No, I'm praying!"

"Oh, you're praying? What are you praying about?" she inquired.

"I'm praying for Mickey's balance and for his sight. I want him to be able to walk again."

Tears pooled in her eyes.

Can you imagine how much more Jud might enjoy Disneyland if God answered our prayers for him, just as he was praying for Mickey Mouse?

Journal Entry: Friday, August 10

Life Unbound

In my opportunities to sit and reflect during this journey, this path the Lord has divinely chosen for me, the importance of gratitude continues to be seared on my heart. When I allow my thoughts, circumstances, and moments to breed discontentment, I find myself discouraged, downtrodden, and unable to cope with the pain that is ever-present. However, when I choose to consider all the amazing wonders that are present in my life, the incredible gifts I have been given, and the joys that shine through even the darkest shadows, I find I am no longer disabled by my wallowing, and my self-pity begins to dissipate; there is freedom to live. It is a posture of thankfulness that delivers me from the abyss.

Is it any wonder, then, why God, in his great care for his beloved, continually encourages us to be thankful? In doing so, he is inviting us to a life unbound by dissatisfaction and entitlement.

I confess that a sincere heart of gratefulness has always been and continues to be a challenge for me. I must discipline my mind. My thoughts must be constrained, where only upon transformation unto gratitude may they be released.

> O give thanks unto the Lord; for he is good:
> For his mercy endureth forever.
>
> O give thanks unto the God of gods:
> For his mercy endureth forever.
>
> O give thanks to the Lord of lords:
> For his mercy endureth forever.
>
> To him who alone doeth great wonders:
> For his mercy endureth forever.
>
> To him that by wisdom made the heavens:
> For his mercy endureth forever.
>
> To him that stretched out the earth above the waters:
> For his mercy endureth forever.
>
> To him that made great lights:
> For his mercy endureth forever.
>
> The sun to rule by day:
> For his mercy endureth forever.
>
> The moon and stars to rule by night:
> For his mercy endureth forever ...
>
> O give thanks unto the God of heaven:
> For his mercy endureth forever.

> *Psalm* 136:1–9, 26 KJV

Journal Entry: Friday, August 10

An Altar

I often wish I had an actual altar where I could lay Jud as an offering to God, literally placing him in Jehovah Jireh's hands that he may do with my boy as he so chooses—so unto his name be all glory and honor. I do not want to withhold Jud. I surrender. May he bend my will as unto his own.

Admittedly, I also pray that he provide a ram in the thicket (Genesis 22:13).

Letter 24: Saturday, August 11

Dear family and friends,

We met with the Make-a-Wish Foundation this morning. What a fantastic organization! They will be trying to organize a vacation for our family very soon. Because Jud is losing his capabilities so quickly, this is considered a "rush wish"—Jud will probably be experiencing his wish sometime in the next couple weeks.

Hoping Jud will enjoy his "wish,"
Christina (on behalf of Drake too)

Journal Entry: Saturday, August 11

Answers

I was reading back through my journals that led right up to the onset of Jud's condition. My heart was truly stirring in preparation for something, though I knew not what.

March 23, 2007: Almost every day, I serve Jud a cereal concoction for breakfast. I take steel-cut oatmeal or seven-grain cereal and add flax seed oil, brewers' yeast, kelp, and milk (I know what you're all thinking—poor kid—well, yes, but he doesn't know the difference; he's had it since he was ten months old). Then I stir it up. I stir it in preparation for his consumption. I started to think about the act of stirring. Ingredients are stirred for the purpose of baking, paint is stirred before it is applied, and substances are stirred for chemistry experiments. Stirring does not seem to be an end in and of itself, but rather a precursor to something else.

My soul is stirring.

I now see that the stirring of my soul was a precursor to this dark valley. However, what truly amazed me, in looking back at my thoughts, is that in and through this particular valley, God has actually answered so many of the prayers I had scrawled in my notebook since the beginning of the year.

I prayed to connect more deeply and relate with others at church. I prayed for Drake and me to have opportunities to use our gifts. I prayed for friendship. I prayed for God to help me "fix my broken thoughts." I prayed for the restoration of strained relationships.

God is answering these prayers and countless others through this dark journey.

There is one prayer I prayed that I am now begging God to answer:

May 19, 2007: Dear Lord, thank you for choosing me to be Jud and Jessie's mom. I am overcome with emotion when I consider what incredible gifts they are—sweet, beautiful, and innocent. Please have mercy on them and protect them. Please guard their hearts and give us wisdom as we seek to honor you in our care for them. Place your hedge around Jud and Jess. Ultimately, may their hearts be yours.

O Father, please hear this prayer!

Month Three:
Developing
Unwavering Faith

Journal Entry: Monday, August 13

Self-help Mechanism

We had our first visit from the hospice doctor today. He was a nice man, showing sensitivity to our circumstances. He asked me how I was coping, and in sharing a little about my journey, I stated that we believe in a God who can miraculously heal Judson, and we are praying to that end.

He later stated that he would support us in whatever spiritual god or entity we needed to believe in that would help us cope with this experience. Though said in kindness, with those few words he leveled Christianity to a mere self-help mechanism.

I am crying out to the Almighty God and Creator of the universe who spoke our world into existence. He breathes life into the lifeless, touches the blind that they may see, enables the lame to walk again, honors the weak and downtrodden, and who sacrificed his only Son, that by grace and forgiveness I can enter into personal relationship with him and ask him to save my only son.

Merely a coping mechanism?

Though I know not what God's ultimate plans are for Judson, a manifestation of his resurrection power would certainly show this doctor and countless others otherwise. Hence, I continue to beseech him accordingly!

Journal Entry: Monday, August 13

Sixty-one Days

Today is exactly two months since Jud's appointment with the doctor that marked the beginning of our experience with this downward spiral in his health—yet it feels like it has been many, many months. When I looked at the calendar today, I was absolutely baffled. Has it really only been 61 days? Each day has felt like the weight of a week or even a month.

Moreover, this means that in just two months, Jud has gone from periodic stumbling with an abnormal gait and intermittently missing his target when he reached for things to being completely immobilized and totally blind, coupled with muscle spasms, fits of pain, extreme irritability, difficulties swallowing, deficits in speech, decreased dexterity in his hands, and more. What a vicious disease!

I am weary.

I am physically run-down and emotionally worn. I do not know how much more I can possibly handle in the day-to-day challenges. There are often moments when the weight feels too heavy, yet I cling to the promise that God will not give me more than I can bear. I desperately need greater strength and hope for this journey.

Please carry my weary soul, O God.

Letter 25: Tuesday, August 14

Dear family and friends,

It looks like the Make-a-Wish Foundation has moved *extremely* quickly, and we will be visiting the Disneyland resort next week. They are throwing us a send-off party on Sunday evening, and then we will be staying for six days and five nights starting Monday. My mom will be watching Jessie at our home, but either she or Sarah will bring her to join us periodically during the week. We are excited! This will provide a great opportunity for the two of us to focus on Jud.

I must admit that I am also apprehensive, seeing as going out with Jud is becoming more and more challenging, and I want him to really enjoy himself. Will you pray for this to be a truly wonderful, enjoyable, and memorable experience for all of us?

This passage has been brought to our attention several times over the last two months and gives us great hope as we pray for Jud. We hope it encourages you too. "I tell you the truth, my Father will give you whatever you ask in my name. Until now you have not asked for anything in my name. Ask and you will receive, and your joy will be complete" (John 16:23b-24).

Much love,
Christina (on behalf of Drake too)

Journal Entry: Tuesday, August 14

Onomatopoeia

Last night was another one of Judson's really difficult evenings in which he struggled to sleep and experienced many fits of screaming (they are becoming more and more frequent). We usually just stand near his bed and stroke his arms, legs, or back and pray over him until he settles.

Sometime after midnight, as he cried out again, I decided to go and lie down next to him in his "big boy" bed. Though he never verbally acknowledged me, he settled down and stopped crying when he sensed my presence. Despite the fact that he had calmed, I couldn't help but linger on his "Lightning McQueen" sheets in the stillness of the night.

After being there for some time, he tossed and turned again, trying to get comfortable, but his eyes remained closed. At one point we ended up lying face-to-face, only inches away; I could feel his warm, sweet breath on my face, and the rhythm of his exhales slowed. He had fallen back asleep in my embrace.

I watched him with awe.

Suddenly and unexpectedly, Jud reached his hands toward me, and as a blind person reads Braille, Jud "read" my face. The tips of his fingers settled on my nose, and with a light squeeze, he broke his verbal silence with, "Honk! Honk!"

Startled and surprised, I began to laugh, which was followed by laughter from my precious boy.

No other words were exchanged between us in the dark, but his onomatopoeia erased the many screams and cries that had come prior.

Journal Entry: Wednesday, August 15

Being In Control

I was challenged by this quote from J. P. Moreland's book Kingdom Triangle:

> Frequently, [Evangelical American Christians] are too cautious and too concerned about "being in control" of all things to get messy and to take risks where you may look foolish if God's manifest presence does not show up. Too often, there is a rigid, controlling, fearful

spirit among you. Too often, you are defensive and stuck in tradition for its own sake. There is too little power in your churches, too little extravagant worship in which your people pour out their hearts to God on Sunday. Too much of your church's accomplishments can be explained without there needing to be a God to explain them. Things are too predictable and too, well, American.[14]

This describes me all too well, but my experience with a genetically, terminally ill child has left me completely "out of control" and grappling with what it means to "get messy and take risks" in my faith.

Journal Entry: Thursday, August 16

Feeble Endurance

We are caught between a rock and a hard place as our day-to-day circumstances become more dire and desperate.

With this disease, we have not yet given Judson any drugs. Our reasons have been twofold. First, one aspect of this disease is the body's inability to release toxins from certain cells (globoid cells). Seeing as drugs are toxic, they can speed progression of symptoms (which we acutely observed after his first MRI anesthesia). Secondly, sedating our boy means less lucid moments and ultimately the loss of some of our most precious intermissions from this ravaging disease, moments when his mind and spirit flourish.

On the flipside, Jud is becoming less and less comfortable, the frequency of pain is increasing, his fits of irritability are almost unbearable, his level of frustration has skyrocketed, and he is no longer sleeping well. Therein, our ability to cope has dramatically diminished. Our tanks are tremendously depleted; we are less comfortable, our pain is increasing, we are frequently irritable, our frustration level is elevated, and our rest is insufficient.

This weight is excruciating and my endurance feeble.

Come, Lord Jesus, in our desperation, please come!

Journal Entry: Friday, August 17

Cry Out

I continuously cry out to God.

> My God, my God, why have you forsaken me? Far from my deliverance are the words of my groaning. O my God, I cry by day, but thou dost not answer; and by night, but I have no rest. But you, O Lord, be not far off; O you my help, hasten to my assistance.

> Deliver our family from Krabbe disease, Jud's life and our lives from the power of this affliction.

> *Psalm* 22:1–2, 19–20 NASB *(personalized)*

Journal Entry: Sunday, August 19

One

Jessie turned one today!

She is such an amazing blessing in our lives. Anyone who has spent any time with me in the last year has probably heard me describe her as "the easiest baby ever!" I truly cannot imagine a more easygoing, go-with-the-flow child. She is such a trooper!

Unless she is hurt, it is extremely rare to hear her cry. She doesn't even so much as whimper when you put her down to sleep but rather jumps up and down in her crib, smiling from ear to ear. When she wakes from her slumber, she just lays in bed cooing until someone comes to get her. When you open the door to her room to retrieve her, she jumps up with a grin, grabs her blanket, and often starts the game of "Peek-a-Boo."

Jessie has been very active from an early age. We call her "squirrelly girly" because she is not one to sit still for very long (we probably need to work on self-control with her). She is physically determined and will let very little get in her way. Where others may choose to go around an obstacle, Jessie will find a way to go through or over it; she will not be hindered. Jessie is fierce in the kindest of ways, and we love that in her!

She has been taking steps for a couple months, but this week she took the plunge and started walking. Seeing as she likes to use the most efficient means of mobility, she still chooses to crawl much of the time, but it is not uncommon to see her walk briskly across the room, especially if her destination is into the arms of someone she loves.

Much like her brother, Jessie is also quite a "talker." Though an interpreter would be quite helpful at this time, she is regularly communicating with us. The sounds she makes are music to my senses.

To look upon Jessie's beautiful face brings pure joy to my heart. It reminds me that life is such an incredible gift and it is important to cherish every moment, for none of us knows what tomorrow may bring.

Today I take special time to consider and treasure my precious Jessie girl who is now one year old. We cannot imagine this season without her!

Journal Entry: Sunday, August 19

Omnipotent

Never before have I felt so powerless.

This week I have watched as my little boy's hands have begun to shrivel. He is almost completely unable to grasp his cup to quench his own thirst or feed himself crackers. Any effort to pick something up is met with great difficulty.

The first time I heard him declare, "My hands are tired," was ten days ago, and now it is commonplace throughout the day.

Yesterday Jud asked me if he could play with his "two-and-a-half-birthday train," so I hunted down the track and set it up for his enjoyment. Then I searched high and low for "Thomas the Tank Engine" and his other friends, at which time Jud requested to play specifically with "James." I placed James on the track, took Jud's hand in my own, and directed it over to his beloved toy for him to "see" its location. He first tried to pick it up but to no avail; then he tried to push it on the track, and it kept falling off. Tears of frustration began to flow. He cried out, "Please play *for* me, Mommy! I can't do it!"

I broke down and began to cry too, feeling inadequate to meet the needs of my boy and bring the touch of healing his body so desperately needs.

But then I realized that though I am, in my humanity, "powerless," I love and serve an omnipotent God, wherein "all that God is, and all that God has, is at the disposal of prayer... Prayer can do anything that God can do, and since God can do anything, prayer is omnipotent" (R. A. Torrey[15]).

So, in fact, I am not powerless but rather can access God's power through prayer.

Letter 26: Monday, August 20

Dear family and friends,

We had Judson's "wish party" thrown by the Make-a-Wish Foundation yesterday at Ruby's Diner, and it was a treat to have the actual "Ruby" and her son who started the franchise come to the party and even give Jud a gift. Jud had a great time and particularly enjoyed the Lightning McQueen ice cream cake and the company of all his cousins! We are now at the Sheraton Hotel in Anaheim to partake in Jud's wish experience. We will keep you posted on our adventure.

Charles Spurgeon once wrote, "We do not need fingertip prayers, which only touch the burden; we need shoulder prayers, which bear a load of earnestness and are not to be denied their desire."[16] We feel like so many of you have covered us in this type of prayer. Thank you!

Much love and gratitude,
Christina (on behalf of Drake too)

Letter 27: Tuesday, August 21

Dear family and friends,

Unfortunately, it was a *very* difficult day. What is intended to be vacation felt rougher than our usual day-to-day. Though there were a couple moments of smiles that we will certainly cherish, Jud was even more uncomfortable, frustrated, and discouraged than usual, which, in turn, meant greater challenge and ultimately much sadness for us. We cannot help but consider how much Jud would be enjoying himself here at the Disney resort if not afflicted by this disease.

Tomorrow is a new day. We would covet your prayers for peaceful rest, strength, endurance, and healing.

Thank you all for your love!

Much gratitude,
Christina (on behalf of Drake too)

Letter 28: Wednesday, August 22

Dear family and friends,

Thank you to all who read our letter yesterday and prayed specifically about our vacation here at Disneyland. Today was one hundred times better than yesterday! Jud had many smiles, some laughter, and a general spirit of contentment; moments of fussiness and frustration were few and far between.

It felt like God was very gracious with us, coming on the heels of a day that felt unbearable in so many ways.

We are so grateful for all your love, support, and prayers! Your words to us help to uphold us and speak truth into our lives. Thank you!

Much love,
Christina (on behalf of Drake too)

Letter 29: Friday, August 24

Dear family and friends,

I wanted to provide another brief Disney vacation update.

Yesterday, day four, was full of many ups and downs, but overall it was generally a decent day. This morning was our best thus far; Jud was in a good mood and even enjoyed a couple of attractions at Disneyland.

This is an e-mail that we received from someone we really don't even know, though he is part of our praying family; it is a great representation of the numerous e-mails we regularly receive that are a tremendous encouragement. Thank you for writing us! May this e-mail be an encouragement to you as well.

Hey, Levasheff family!

My wife, Kelly, and I are constantly praying for you. I have been suffering in prayer for you and spending the majority of my prayer time calling God to work his power in Judson and in your lives and bodies as parents. You must be weary, and I know you need prayer.

I am calling on God to act on his compassion, to reverse Judson's symptoms, and to destroy the disease altogether. I believe he will. The reason I believe he will is that I must believe it. The greatest thing I ever learned from reading John Piper was that God is a God of future grace. He wants my faith to be the kind of faith that is sure of what he will do in his love.

Therefore, I look forward to each new minute, knowing that every next moment could be the turning point upward for Judson! Science and human understanding are simply nothing when it comes to the power of God. Though I suffer hour by hour with you and Judson, I have great hope, knowing that every minute is in God's hands. At any moment, I can be eagerly expectant of Judson's healing because I believe God will do it.

So I want to join my hope with yours, looking forward to God's future grace. If Jesus ever had compassion on anyone, I know he has great compassion on Judson, and his dear, loving, weary parents.

Grace and peace to you as we continue wrestling in prayer for your precious son.

Timothy Pinkham

We appreciate all of you,
Christina (on behalf of Drake too)

Journal Entry: Friday, August 24

Smaller Things

We are being challenged to trust God in prayer for smaller things, even things that may seem somewhat insignificant, as we petition him for Jud's healing.

The Make-a-Wish organization booked a single room with two queen beds for our family. Seeing as Jud is now a very fitful sleeper and often screams out many times throughout the night, though still asleep, we knew we wouldn't get any sleep ourselves if we were in the same room with him for five nights. Therefore, before we left on our trip, Drake prayed specifically for God to open the door for us to be in some type of suite without having to pay any additional money.

When we arrived at the hotel, Drake communicated our situation to the front desk personnel and requested to be upgraded to a room situation where we could have two adjacent areas with a connecting door. The employees informed us that this type of upgrade was absolutely impossible and there were no suitable rooms available. At this point, Drake offered to pay for the upgrade; it was essential for us! The woman at the front desk decided to get the manager. After hearing our situation, the manager, without hesitation, upgraded us to the "Turret Suite," the best type of room in this hotel, free of charge (even after Drake had offered to pay)!

This answer to prayer was an encouragement and helped to increase our faith.

Journal Entry: Saturday, August 25

Dreams

Earlier this evening I held in my hand a complimentary lanyard from our Make-a-Wish vacation that read, "Disneyland: Where All Your Dreams Come True." My mind was gripped with grief, knowing that our dream, day and night, is to have Jud's body restored to wholeness, and Disneyland seemed to actually accentuate the increased disability in his body.

Sadly, the "Happiest Place on Earth" held very little for him. In his blind, almost quadriplegic state, he was left to simply enjoy sounds and familiar concepts. Everything else seemed to overwhelm his senses.

However, there were moments of smiles and laughter that are branded in my memory. "It's a Small World" was probably the biggest highlight (which is ironic, seeing as it has always been my least favorite attraction at Disneyland)! We boarded the turquoise-trimmed boats each day we visited the park, and every time, about three-fourths of the way through the ride, a smile emerged on Jud's face, and he began to "clap" to the music.

Though our motives were somewhat selfish, we were able to convince Jud to ride the new Nemo submarine ride, and he actually enjoyed listening to Dori and Nemo (one of the few movies he has ever seen). In fact, he enjoyed it so much that he asked to ride it the next day, and on his second experience, he was extremely proud to sit in his own seat all by himself (the smallest of things are now huge accomplishments!).

Seeing as Jud adores trains, we rode a couple different trains: the "Casey Jr. Circus Train," the steam engine that goes around the park, the "Bug's Life" train, and the monorail. He liked the concept that he was riding a train, yet because of his blindness and little auditory stimuli on these attractions, they left a little something to be desired. In fact, he was just as enthusiastic about riding the shuttle that took us to and from the hotel; he affectionately named it "Bertie the Bus" (one of Thomas the Tank Engine's friends).

Disney actually provides a "Wish Lounge" for Make-a-Wish kids to rest and relax throughout the day, which included refreshments and snacks. Without question, this was Jud's favorite thing at Disneyland; we spent the bulk of our time there. In fact, they even invited Mickey and Minnie Mouse, along with Pinocchio, to spend some one-on-one time with Jud; though Jud had never heard of Pinocchio before, he really enjoyed playing with the Disney mice and the puppet who became a boy.

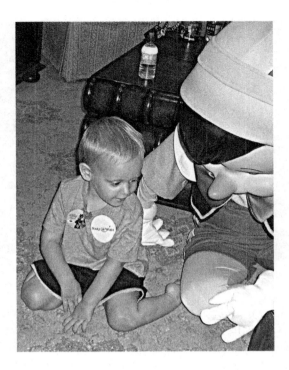

Our trip also included a breakfast at "Goofy's Kitchen," a restaurant where Disney characters mingle with the guests. Jud was a little out-of-sorts that morning, but each time a character came to our table, we were touched by the joy that covered his face.

Though our dreams did not necessarily come true at Disneyland, they can come to life by the touch of our Creator God. In turn, Jud's next trip to Disneyland could be filled with the anticipation and excitement of a fully capable little boy.

Letter 30: Monday, August 27

Dear family and friends,

We are weary. This vicious disease is plaguing us both day and night and taxing our bodies and souls. There have been many moments we feel too weak to pray, and it is simply our sighs, moans, and cries that reach the ears of God Almighty. I think God is using so many of you to pray *for* us. Thank you!

In all this, we continue to hope in a God who moves supernaturally, and we wait. We wait expectantly! In the waiting, we surrender our hearts, asking the Lord to bend our will as unto his own.

We are tremendously grateful for the numerous ways that you continue to uphold us.

Much love,
Christina (on behalf of Drake too)

Journal Entry: Monday, August 27

Rejected Embrace

This evening Judson was sitting on his knees (the only position he can now maintain on his own) and trying to hoist himself into the beanbag chair in his room. But due to the loss of strength in his arms and legs, he missed his target, tumbled to the side, and fell prone on the floor, completely unable to get up. Understandably, screams of frustration ensued.

I moved quickly to his aid, scooping him into my arms, setting him upright again, and trying to hold and comfort him in his time of great need. Yet instead of leaning into my embrace, he yelled, "Please don't touch me!" (We read somewhere that kids with this disease sometimes do not like to be touched.)

"But, Judson, I want to hold and comfort you. Please let me hold you," I petitioned in brokenness.

"No, Mommy. Please stop!" he cried, using his debilitated arms to try and push me aside.

"I think you need comfort, Judson. I want to love you up." I hugged him even more tightly.

An awful shrill escaped his lungs.

I let go. I scooted backward and collapsed on the floor, crushed.

I crave any opportunity to enfold Jud into my embrace, yet sometimes he rejects my efforts.

As I sat on the floor next to my broken boy, immediately after this encounter, it struck me—have I been responding to God in much the same way that Jud just responded to me? Is my heavenly Father trying to hold me in my pain and frustration, but I keep pushing him away?

May it never be so! Oh Lord, please scoop me up in your arms. Please hold and comfort me. I desperately need you!

Journal Entry: Tuesday, August 28

Unheard

One of the things I have come to recognize over the years in my relationship with Drake is that I hate feeling unheard. I am highly sensitive in this area (and many other areas too). When it feels like Drake is not understanding me or not listening to what I am trying to communicate, an alarm sounds in my being, and my ire is raised. This knee-jerk response, which is grounded in hurt, is likely related to my family of origin (sorry Mom and Dad). Whatever the case may be, every time I experience feeling unheard, it strikes me at the very core.

In our current circumstance, I feel like my cries to God are not being heard. Day and night, I call out to him to release our family from this affliction, and yet it gets harder and harder with each passing moment. It is agonizing.

Are you listening, dear God? Do you hear me? In my most honest reflections, I feel tinges of anger toward you. I don't want to feel this way, for in my mind I know I am not entitled to anything, but in my heart I am desperate for you to hear me and answer my cries. It hurts to feel unheard.

> Save me, O God, for the waters have threatened my life. I have sunk in deep mire, and there is no foothold; I have come into deep waters, and a flood overflows me. I am weary with my crying;

my throat is parched; my eyes fail while I wait for my God.

My prayer is to you, O Lord, at an acceptable time; O God, in the greatness of your loving-kindness, answer me with your saving truth. Deliver me from the mire, and do not let me sink.

Answer me, O Lord, for your lovingkindness is good: according to the greatness of your compassion, turn to me. And do not hide your face from your servant, for I am in distress; answer me quickly.

Psalm 69:1–3, 13–14, 16–17 NASB

I am afflicted and needy; hasten to me, O God! You are my help and my deliverer; O Lord, do not delay.

Psalm 70:5 NASB

Journal Entry: Wednesday, August 29

Speechless

As I sit in solitude this morning, I realize that my heart feels like it is slowly being wrenched out of my chest, bit by bit, but I can hardly cry anymore; the tears regularly just sit in my eyes on the brink of flowing downward but too exhausted to make the journey. Moreover, no lamentation seems to sufficiently communicate or express the sorrow in my soul—words feel empty, lacking ability to adequately represent my inner world.

Yet, I still sit here, trying to write, trying to purge my innermost thoughts and feelings, hoping that somehow it will cleanse my mind and serve as the catharsis it has often been.

Unfortunately, this morning, I remain speechless. Ugh!

Letter 31: Thursday, August 30

Dear family and friends,

I wanted to provide another brief update on Jud's symptoms. Jud is only able to maintain one position on his own: sitting on his knees. However, in the last two days he has been regularly falling from that position; it is probably not long before he will need to be lying down all the time or in a seat with restraints. He has lost all dexterity in his hands and can no longer pick up anything. Furthermore—and this is the most gripping for us—he has been dramatically losing his ability to speak in the last week; it is often that we cannot understand him.

Dear God, please heal Judson from this insidious disease!

With sorrow, yet hope too,
Christina (on behalf of Drake too)

Thursday, August 30

letter **by Tamie Vervoorn**

Dear friends and family of the Levasheffs,

We're inviting you to join us in an all-night prayer vigil this Monday, September 3, as a labor of love for Judson and the Levasheff/Adelseck family. Together we are believing God to completely heal and restore Judson's body and soul and to bring strong encouragement to his family.

We know that God works mightily when believers gather together in Jesus' name and when we agree together to ask him for anything. Although we might be scattered throughout the states—and the world—we can gather together in spirit (and in cyberspace!) to make this happen. Will you join us in laboring for Judson's life on Monday, September 3?

Remember that we serve a compassionate, all-knowing, all-powerful God, who demonstrated his love for us in his only Son, Jesus Christ. It is by his wounds that we are healed and by his blood that we have forgiveness and the hope of eternal life. As Isaiah says,

> Surely our griefs/[sickness] he himself bore, and our sorrows he carried; yet we ourselves esteemed him stricken, smitten of God, and afflicted. But he was pierced through for our transgressions, he was crushed for our iniquities; the chastening for our well-being fell upon him and by his scourging we are healed.
>
> *Isaiah* 53:4–5 NASB

With much gratitude, faith, and anticipation,
Friends of Judson

Journal Entry: Friday, August 31

Taste and See

The Psalms have been speaking to my heart significantly during this season. Psalm 34 is one that I go back to again and again. These are some of my reflections interspersed with the passage.

This poor man cried and the Lord heard him,

Please heal Jud!

And saved him out of all his troubles.

Please deliver our family from this affliction!

The angel of the Lord encamps around those who fear him,

Please protect us.

And rescues them.

Come, dear Lord, and save us!

O taste and see that the Lord is good;

O God, I know it to be true!

How blessed is the man who takes refuge in him!

I want my strength and hope to be found in you.

O fear the Lord, you his saints;

Please show me any darkness in my soul.

For those who fear him, there is no want.

I am in want; I desire health for my son!

The young lions do lack and suffer hunger; But they who seek the Lord shall not be in want of any good thing.

I desire you to heal Jud and believe it to be a good thing.

Come, you children, listen to me;

My ear is inclined to you.

I will teach you the fear of the Lord.
Who is the man who desires life,
And loves length of days
that he may see good?

*Please give Jud many days that he may continue
to bless your name here on earth.*

Psalm 34:6–12 NASB

Journal Entry: Sunday, September 2

An Enormous Raft

I received an e-mail today from someone I have never met, Kristy Harrang, who heard about our story through a mutual friend and has been praying for us the last couple weeks. She wrote something that gave me cause to pause:

> One joy that I see for you in the midst of all of your sorrow and heartache is that you have an opportunity to experience his comfort and grace to a degree that few others will ever understand in this lifetime.

What an incredible and beautiful thought!

God has truly been heaping his comfort and grace upon us. We can almost bask in it each day, like one who cannot swim might be buoyed by a raft and may even choose to lounge in a pool, soaking in the sunshine. Without the raft, they would be in great peril; yet, beyond serving as a life-saving aid, the raft actually enables the potential for pleasure in a situation that might otherwise place them in jeopardy.

Prior to this circumstance, we had never learned how to swim in grief or tragedy, but the Lord has placed us on his enormous raft of comfort and grace, whereby we have additionally found gifts and joys in our trial.

Monday, September 3

Reflections on the Story of Lazarus
by Drake Levasheff

I've been thinking a lot about Jesus' raising of Lazarus (John

11:1–46) recently and finally took some time to reflect on it over the past day or so.

So the story begins. Upon receiving word that Lazarus is ill, Jesus declares, "This sickness will not end in death. No, it is for God's glory so that God's Son may be glorified through it" (John 11:4). His words provide a framework for reading the entire passage: God has a purpose in this and will display his glory and will glorify his Son. There are many reasons that God heals people; in the case of John's gospel, it is usually for the glory of God and his Son (cf. John 9).

As I have prayed for Judson's healing, the glory of God has never been far from my mind. I have thought about what it would mean to the doctors and nurses who have treated Jud. I have thought about what it would mean to unsaved friends and family members. I have thought about what it would mean to members of the family of faith all over the world. As I have pictured Jud before each of these groups, restored to health, I can't help but rejoice because I see how greatly God would be glorified, and I grow in expectancy for such a work. And only he can be glorified, because only he can do this!

As the story continues, John makes it clear how much Jesus loves Lazarus and his sisters, Mary and Martha. "Jesus loved Martha and her sister and Lazarus" (John 11:5). And he loves all of us in the community of faith as well. We've sensed that love over this period; Jesus loves Jud and cares tenderly for him and us!

But love doesn't stop Jesus from doing things that confound those he loves. John 11:6 says, "Yet when he heard that Lazarus was sick, he stayed where he was two more days." On the heels of Jesus' declared love for Lazarus and his sisters, this statement is striking: Having heard Lazarus is sick, he stays in the same place two days longer! Why would he delay with those he loves? Knowing how much the Lord loves Jud and us, we have wondered the same thing.

For Martha and Mary, delay means death of their loved one. And so when Jesus arrives, both sisters say to him, "Lord, if you had been here, my brother would not have died" (John 11:21, 32). It's hard not to read disappointment in their voices. It's not just that they thought he could have done something; it's easy to infer that they were disappointed that he was not there. They sent word to someone who loved them in their desperate need. And he took his time getting there.

And anyone in their circumstance might then question his love: "If you do love us, why would you delay in coming?" This resonates with me. I have long believed that the Lord intends to heal Jud, but the waiting has been awful. His deterioration is so hard to watch. He is frustrated so often. And his suffering has engulfed us. So we have asked, "How long will you delay, O Lord?"

Though Jesus delays his arrival, it does not mean that he is untouched by our grief and sorrow. "When Jesus saw [Mary] weeping and the Jews who had come along with her also weeping, he was deeply moved in spirit and troubled" (John 11:33). When he saw Lazarus' gravesite, he wept (John 11:35). Jesus is touched by our suffering; God came near enough to our sorrows to be moved by them. This is a comforting thought!

We all know how the story ends. Jesus calls Lazarus out from the grave (John 11:43–44). The family he loves receives a brother back to life, many believe in Jesus as a result, and the Son of God is glorified in it. And that glory is greater because Jesus waited—there would be no dispute that Lazarus was dead and no doubt that Jesus had called one back from the grave.

So we are in much the same place as Mary and Martha were. Medical science has declared a death sentence over Jud. All the while we have cried out for and expected God's healing—and so have many people along with us! But God has delayed. And so we have painfully witnessed another month of Jud's decline. But in that time, God has been working, touching hearts and bringing in others to share in Jud's suffering and ours. His work by his Spirit has been evident!

Still, his deliverance is coming, for he hears the prayers of his people and stretches forth his hand to heal. And when God rains down his deliverance on Jud, the joy and glory will redound all the more because he waited!

Please continue to pray with us to that end!

Letter 32: Tuesday, September 4

Dear family and friends,

Last night when I went to bed, I read this quote, and it has stuck with me all day today.

> How important it is for God to keep us focused on things that are unseen, for we are so easily snared by the things we can see! ... God is teaching us [that] he has to keep results that are encouraging away from us until we learn to trust him without them. Then he loves to make his Word as real to us in actuality as it is in our faith.
>
> *A. B. Simpson*[17]

Jud is spending most of his days lying in bed now. The last two days he has not had much of an appetite (though he ate pretty well tonight), and we are having difficulty getting him to drink his liquids. It was hard to hear the hospice nurse tell me today that this is "a sign of the body starting to shut down." We're not sure that's the case, but nonetheless we pray for God to continue to foster a spirit of strength and determination in Jud.

We would covet your prayers for our extended family as well. The stress of this situation is significantly affecting them too.

Much love,
Christina (on behalf of Drake too)

Journal Entry: Tuesday, September 4

Faith and Hope

Now faith is being sure of what we hope for and certain of what we do not see.

Hebrews 11:1

One of the things that Drake and I have chosen to do during this season—and it tends to increase our faith—is ponder what life will be like when Jud is delivered from Krabbe disease and his body is restored.

We hope by visualizing Jud jumping out of bed in the morning, running into our arms, looking us in the eyes, and clearly articulating, "I love you!"

We hope by thinking about the letter we will write to family and friends when Jud's body is touched by God's resurrection power and he is healed. We discuss the phone calls that will ensue and dream of people's responses.

We hope by envisioning the enormous "Celebration of Life and the Living God" party that we will throw upon his deliverance. We talk about all the people we would want to be there, especially the many we have never met who have been standing with us in faith. We talk about possible venues, music, and events that might transpire.

We hope by picturing our family on another Disney vacation and imagining all the things that Jud will enjoy after regaining his sight and mobility. His passion for cars will come alive on "Autopia," he will actually see Nemo and Dori while traveling on the submarine rather than just hear them, he will point out the butterflies and other flying objects on "Small World," he will be able to hug Mickey, and he will have to wait in line because he will no longer need a "Guest Assistance" card.

We hope when we look at the park directly outside our windows and consider the joy we will have when Jud runs across the grass again, climbs the ladders, and slides down the slide into our arms. Oh, how fun it will be to see him, once again, go up to the other kids in the park and ask, "What's your name?"

We hope by imagining how incredible it will be to have Jud walking beside us, hand-in-hand, as we visit people who have labored with us in faith, at church, at work, in our hometowns, and all over the globe. None of us will ever be the same.

Now faith, the kind of faith God is fostering in us, is being sure, being confident of these things. "Faith is the assurance of things hoped for…" Though they are not yet visible, we think and speak of them with certainty. Faith is "the conviction of things not seen" (Hebrews 11:1, NASB).

To God be the glory! Amen!

Journal Entry: Wednesday, September 5

Beautiful

I was putting Judson to bed last night, and as he lay there, his eyelids getting heavy, I placed my arms on his bedrail, upon which I rested my head, and gazed upon his face. I observed his breath as his chest steadily rose and fell. He had no idea I was still there.

I thought about his personality, his sense of humor, his sharp mind, and his developing character. I dreamed of the man he might become.

After a couple minutes, it appeared he had fallen asleep.

I continued to sit in awe. What an incredible blessing to have this wonderful boy as our son! Being so moved by my thoughts, I whispered aloud, "You're so beautiful! You're just so beautiful!"

Though his eyes remained closed, a huge smile formed on his face.

Surprised that he was awake, I whispered, "Good night, my little Jud Bud. Sleep well," as I kissed that precious smile.

As I shut the door to his room and began to walk down the stairs, I realized that my heavenly Father looks down on me (as he does with all his children), and even in all my frailty and brokenness he declares, "You're so beautiful! You're just so beautiful!"

My countenance beamed with a smile.

Journal Entry: Saturday, September 8

A Peek behind Closed Doors

It happened again today. I was sobbing so hard that I started retching, staring down into the plastic Target bag my mom had quickly handed to me. There have been a couple times over the last months that I get so worked up crying that my body starts purging. I can't seem to control it.

When I am out and about at church, playgroup, the grocery store, or running errands, I often have people comment on my strength during this season, at which point I usually say something like, "Oh, you just aren't aware of what I'm like at home, but thank you." When I walk away from the conversation, all my moments of weakness, frustration, and pain flood my mind. I think to myself, *They have no idea what my life is like behind closed doors.*

I want to be genuine. But am I?

My most raw moments rarely occur with an audience. I don't think I am consciously choosing to be inauthentic; it's more about appropriateness of time and place. I am also not nearly as gripped by my circumstances when I am selecting ripe bananas compared to when I am at home and Jud has been crying non-stop for three hours, not taking his much-needed nap.

How do you live authentically in hardship while maintaining "normal," day-to-day activities?

Yesterday I started yelling at the top of my lungs, "I can't take it anymore! I can't do this!" over and over again until I was hoarse. Afterward I was worried that the neighbors might have heard me.

Though I express desire to be genuine, maybe, in actuality, I am still trying to make sure that what's behind closed doors stays behind closed doors.

Journal Entry: Sunday, September 9

Dealing with a "Death Sentence"

Having hope for your child to be restored to wholeness by the living God after receiving a "death sentence" from health professionals elicits many diverse responses from people.

Though never stated outright, I sense that some people may think we're a little nuts! We're talking about supernatural healing, and unless one believes there is a God and that he moves miraculously in the lives of his people, then we probably do seem a little kooky. We've decided we're okay with that.

There are others who feel sorry for us. They expect Jud will die (whether it be because of past personal experience or unbelief), and because we've believed Jud will be healed, they don't want us to be even more disappointed "when he passes"—they want to protect us from greater pain by preparing us for loss. We appreciate their concern but recognize the risk we are taking; we still choose to hope in God's supernatural healing power (something that is admittedly foreign to us prior to this experience into which we have been thrust).

Still, there are probably others who think we may be living in denial (mostly health care professionals). We have not faced the fact that our son has a "terminal" disease. They perceive that we are not dealing directly with the issue at hand. On the contrary, one cannot spend even a couple hours with Jud without being convinced that he is on a path toward death. We know it. We see it. We experience it every day. However, we have hope that God will halt and reverse this path.

Many believers are quick to remind us that it may not be God's will to heal Jud. I know some of these people are simply encouraging us to surrender our will to our Sovereign God. Yes, Lord! Please reveal your perfect will to us. Interestingly, as we pray this, we become more convinced that God is calling us to plead for our son's healing.

I also perceive that when others remind us that it might not be God's will to heal Jud, they are "protecting" God just in case he doesn't "show up." Because we have believed so strongly that God will heal Jud and have proclaimed it to so many, they don't want to risk having God look "impotent" if Jud dies. We are confident God can take care of his own reputation; his will cannot be thwarted, and his plans are perfect. As we incline our ears to him and pray for Jud's healing, may it be that we are actually partnering with him for his good work.

I know of others who have a fear that our faith as believers will falter if Jud passes away, since we have believed God would do otherwise; there is concern that our trust in the Lord of heaven and earth cannot bear such weight. I hope and presume that our journey with our Father is strong enough to withstand anything, but we definitely need to be prudent in this area. Certainly, questions would arise if Jud is not delivered, but I suspect, whatever the outcome, it will bring a deepening of our faith.

Many have believed for a period of time that God would heal Jud, but as time passes and Jud's symptoms progress, it becomes harder to have faith for deliverance. Every indicator, from a human standpoint, declares that Jud is dying. It is hard not to have these outward signs shape our perspective. However, we do not know God's timing. Rather than allow this extended duration of suffering to discourage us, we want it to bring more resolve, cause us to press in deeper to the heart of God, and strengthen our fervency.

We are so blessed to have many who continue to stand with us in faith. Daily they are encouraging our expectancy to see God move miraculously. They are praying with us. They are delving into Scripture with us. They are worshipping with us. They are sacrificing for us. Furthermore, they testify to us each day that they become more convinced that the Spirit of God is alive and moving in this situation, and God is calling them, just as he has been calling us, to pray for Jud and our family to be released from this affliction. God uses these people, many whom we have never even met, to uphold us in our faith! What an incredible blessing!

We do not know the final outcome for our son, but whatever the response of others may be, God is calling me to foster an unwavering faith that chooses to believe the "impossible" before it is seen. I want to be faithful.

Journal Entry: Sunday, September 9

Comfort Zone

I played basketball throughout my elementary years, junior high, high school, and even intramural basketball in college. Though man-to-man defense was most commonly practiced on the court, I was a fan of zone defense. I was a guard, and zone defense allowed me to remain at the top of the key without having to "throw some elbows" in the lane under the hoop; it permitted me to stay in my comfort zone, so to speak, on the court.

I like staying in my comfort zone.

I am recently realizing how much our circumstances with Jud have not just pushed me out of my spiritual comfort zone but rather hurled me into a new world of belief and understanding of who God is and how he works in the lives of his people.

I come from a very conservative Christian background, one in which I have "believed" that God can move miraculously, but in practice and experience assumed it to be extremely infrequent. Admittedly, I have even shied away from such things because of my tweaked perception that most people who describe seeing God work through "signs and wonders" are counterfeits.

I have been living a life of unbelief.

Early on in this process with Jud, I had been challenged with this passage from Mark 9:14–29.

> A father asked Jesus to heal his son, "If you can do anything, take pity on us and help us," he cried.
>
> "*If* you can?" said Jesus. "Everything is possible for him who believes."
>
> Immediately the boy's father exclaimed, "I do believe; help me overcome my unbelief!"
>
> *Mark* 9:14–29

Since that time, I have continually called out to God, "Please help me overcome my unbelief!" And I believe he has been doing just that. The Lord has brought numerous people and resources into my life that have been significantly challenging me and encouraging my faith. I am gaining a new dependence on the Spirit of God and expectancy that he moves powerfully in and through his people.

These words from Dallas Willard resonate with me:

> I go to churches all the time where the people's hunger for piety is enormously high, but they live in constant frustration because they don't have the accompanying faith that God really could change who they are—because they never see signs of God doing things. If you want to have faith, if you want to have faith for changed lives, you have to maintain the visible signs of the Holy Spirit.[18]

I am realizing that being stretched out of my spiritual comfort zone is essential for God to do a new and fresh work in my soul.

Letter 33: Monday, September 10

Dear family and friends,

This last week has been, without question, our most difficult week yet. Not only were we dealing with the usual concerns surrounding Jud, but Jessie was ill for a couple of days, and then we had significant issues emerge with our extended family. There are definitely moments when it feels like the trials are being heaped on us.

That being said, we also experienced some significant graces too. This weekend, my parents temporarily moved into a wonderful, fully furnished home nearby us. It is only six miles from our home. We also had some neat visits with friends this week, and God has been using others to open our eyes as to how we can pray more specifically in our current circumstances. These are truly gifts to us during this season!

Jud can't maintain any position on his own now and isn't even able to sit in his booster seat anymore; he lacks the strength and balance in his neck and torso to hold himself up. His arms and legs don't function much at all now. Most of the time he lays in bed, on the couch, in the beanbag, or on a special chair we purchased for him this week. Yet we still go for walks in the stroller, he enjoys taking drives in the car, and he loves an occasional dip in the Jacuzzi. His great-est pleasures now come from listening to books on tape, kid's radio programs, or from using his imagination to play.

His speech is rapidly deteriorating. It is so hard to under-stand much of what he says, but we hate to have him keep repeating himself because he is already so frustrated. It is truly heartbreaking!

His sleep was abysmal this last week, both during naps and at night. However, yesterday and today have been better.

His appetite ebbs and flows, so we are quite pleased when he eats a good meal.

Activity in the body is necessary for bowel health, and because Jud is now unable to move much, it is starting to create difficulty in his digestive system.

Jud's mind remains very sharp!

We try to put ourselves in Jud's shoes but cannot even begin to imagine what it must be like to feel trapped inside a body that is shutting down.

Thank you for your continued support and prayers,
Christina (on behalf of Drake too)

Monday, September 10

Letter **by Rebekah Davenport**

Dear praying family of Judson Levasheff,

This is an invitation to join in a time of prayer for Jud and his family, to fervently ask our compassionate God for healing and restoration for Judson and strength for Drake and Christina (and their extended family as well). Let's ask him to reveal his perfect will and to bring glory to himself in the outcome of this heartbreaking disease.

If fifty to one-hundred of us join together in a commitment to pray for fifteen to thirty minutes daily, we will be able to cover Judson and his family in prayer twenty-four hours a day.

This will be a great comfort to Drake and Christina during sleepless nights, Judson's tears (and their own), and moments of anxiety and sorrow. At every moment of the day, they will be able to rest assured that one of us is in prayer for them.

Although Judson's illness has brought great sorrow to many of us, we are convinced that God means it for good. Let's commit together to be faithful to God's calling to "pray for one another." Although we are spread around the world, by giving of ourselves in prayer, we can have the awesome privilege of showing our love for the Levasheff family and participating in God's work in their lives.

Your sister in Christ,
Rebekah Davenport

Journal Entry: Monday, September 10

Medical vs. Miraculous

There was national media attention given several months ago to a family with a son who was battling cancer; the parents wanted to opt out of giving their son another round of chemotherapy treatment. People were up in arms that his folks would not pursue every possible medical means available to keep their son alive.

There is absolutely no medical cure available to treat the vicious disease that has overtaken Judson's body. Jud's only "treatment" must come from the touch of the living God.

The irony is that many people were up in arms when a family refused certain medical treatments for their son, but when we choose to seek "treatment" for our son by the Giver of Life, many discourage us from it (even some Christians—though rarely overtly).

Have we really come to rely on and accept medical science over the miraculous power of God?

Journal Entry: Wednesday, September 12

Juxtaposing My J's

Jessie is now able to walk everywhere.

I was in the living room with the two kids the other evening. Jud was sitting in my lap, and Jessie was walking "circles" around us as she moved from toy to toy with great pride and pleasure. Out of the blue, Jud asked with a somber voice, "Is Jessie walking?"

I perceived it to be a weighty question. "Yes, Jud, Jessie is walking," I responded with great sensitivity.

Jud just sat there with a pensive, almost downcast, look on his face. I sensed he had just encountered greater realization of his deficiencies. I saw his pain and felt pain for him.

Jessie just learned to clap last week.

We were playing an audio story for Judson this afternoon, and when the music began, Jessie started to clap, which, of course, was met with effusive praise. When I turned back to Jud, I became aware that he was mustering up every bit of strength to bring his hands together so he too could clap. His index fingers barely touched, and with my realization, I heaped on praise at his accomplishment. He smiled.

Jessie is starting to talk.

The other day I was handing Jessie objects and pronouncing with as much clarity as possible the name of each one. Then I would ask Jessie to repeat the word. Periodically she seemed to articulate a sound that was fairly similar to the actual word, so I would clap and say, "Good job, Jessie!" The next thing I know, Jud, in his fractured speech, tried to articulate the same word, longing to receive similar accolades. Praise for my sweet boy flowed.

Jessie is gaining so many new abilities, which is such a joy to watch. Meanwhile, Judson is losing all his capabilities. To juxtapose the two elicits greater anguish on behalf of my little man.

Month Four:
Risking with
Expectant Hope

Letter 34: Thursday, September 13

Dear family and friends,

I sit here writing this journal, acutely aware that 'round-the-clock prayer commenced for our family. It moves me to tears. Rebekah shared with us that over sixty-five people were eager to set aside time each day to specifically pray for our family. We are truly humbled and blessed. Thank you!

We also know that there are *so* many others praying regularly for us, and we cannot express enough gratitude to our ever-growing praying family. We know God hears and is moved by the collective prayers of his people.

I cannot reiterate enough how the love and support of everyone who reads these letters is enabling us to bear up under our current circumstances and walk this path. Please know that we not only read every word you write us, we digest them. At times we even thirst for them like water for our soul (this may sound dramatic but is nonetheless true). Everything written to us is cherished and appreciated! Thank you.

Though Jud's physical symptoms continue to decline, his disposition has improved quite a bit this last week—he has been more content from moment to moment with less outbursts of pain and frustration and more smiles. It has made it easier to care for him. We are grateful!

Much love and gratitude,
Christina (on behalf of Drake too)

Journal Entry: Thursday, September 13

Darkness Cannot (and Will Not) Prevail

Sadly I must admit that I am finding it difficult to spend time alone with Jud now. I am overcome with such significant pain, grief, sadness, and discouragement that I am almost swallowed up by the darkness. This disease is evil! Mind you, God may have allowed Krabbe to afflict our family, and I know without question that he is using it and will use it for good, but the disease, in and of itself, feels like it is right out of the pit of hell. It is torture. It is torture for Jud, and it is torture for all of us watching him suffer.

Lest I be swallowed up by the darkness, I must consciously choose to live in the light.

When I spend time reading the promises of God, praying, journaling, and meditating on Scripture, I truly have a peace that surpasses my understanding. The Lord uses it to guard my heart and mind against the darkness that seeks to entangle me. In order to survive this journey, every thought must be taken captive. I want my mind to be steadfast on the one who calls me beloved, that I may hold firmly to the truth and allow the Word to take root in my soul.

Where there is light, there can be no darkness. I cannot allow darkness to prevail—so let there be light in my life!

Journal Entry: Friday, September 14

Two Broken Bodies

My parents are staying in a duplex on Balboa Island in Newport Beach (thank you Hogans!). The people who live above them have a cat named Oliver. Ollie is aged; he is a quadriplegic and mute kitty.

We went to visit my mom today on the island, and she asked Jud if he wanted Oliver to come visit. Jud was enthusiastic about the prospect.

As Judson lay stiff on the couch, Michael, Ollie's "daddy," came and laid Oliver next to Jud. Jud's eyes and face brightened with a huge smile.

He had a buddy!

Jud wanted to share everything he had with Oliver. In his broken voice, Jud asked Oliver if he liked his monster truck, and he wanted Oliver to touch the big wheels. Then he wanted Oliver to play with his red racecar. As I moved Jud's hands to touch Oliver's nose, legs, and head, Michael was moving Ollie's paw to touch Judson's arm.

There they lay—two broken bodies.

"Judson, did you know that Oliver's body doesn't work properly either? He is not able to walk, or run, or jump," I informed my precious boy with a diseased body.

"I want to make him better, Mommy!" Jud stated with significantly slurred speech. "I want him to be better."

Every eye in the room pooled with tears.

Judson is extremely aware of his deficits, which lead to great frustration, sadness, and pain. But I love that he has the sensitivity to never want anyone else, even a kitty, to be trapped in a body that doesn't function properly.

Just as he expressed to Oliver, I regularly think to myself, "I want to make you better, Judson! I want you to be better."

Journal Entry: Friday, September 14

Inside Jud's Head

Jud's whole body is now paralyzed. Therefore, when we put him to bed we try to lay him in a comfortable position and hope it will last the whole night. If he gets uncomfortable, he has no way of moving himself; screams of frustration often ensue.

Last night was a difficult night. Judson had been awake for more than five hours, intermittently crying and screaming. It was 3:30 a.m. when Drake "passed the baton" to me for the second time.

I went into Jud's room as his screams grew louder and louder. Not knowing how to comfort him, I asked, "Can I hold you?" Thrilled by his affirmative response, I scooped him up in my arms and held him tightly. After a few minutes, he began to calm down. Once he was no longer sobbing, I investigated. "Why were you crying so much, Bud Bud?"

"I can't roll over, Mommy!" he expressed with his garbled voice.

"I am so sorry, Judson. I am so sorry!" I replied as my heart sank, not really knowing what words I could say to comfort him in his frustration over his crippled frame.

Fortunately, Jud had already moved on in the conversation.

"I have a racecar for you," he declared.

I sensed he was trying to lift his arm as if to give me something, but seeing as there was nothing in his hand, I realized I had just entered the world of his imagination, which is now his greatest pleasure.

"Oh, thank you, Jud."

"No, Mommy. It is in a package. You need to open it."

"Oh, wow! A surprise, Judson? Thank you!" I exclaimed as I made noises that might indicate I was opening a package. "It's a race car!" I declared, and then added, "A blue race car! Thank you so much! I've never seen such a neat race car before!"

"I have one too, Mommy. Will you open it?"

"Of course!" I responded as I tried to duplicate the sounds I had previously made while opening the first package. "What did you get, Judson?"

"A race car. Mine is number twelve," Jud announced with excitement.

"Really? What number is my race car?"

"Yours is number three. Daddy has a racecar too. His is number one."

"Wow! Daddy would really like to be number one!" I replied, knowing Drake would have chuckled had he been there.

"What color is your racecar, Jud?" I questioned, trying to continue engaging his imagination.

"It's blue. Daddy's is blue too."

"Wow! We all have blue racecars: numbers twelve, three, and one. That is so cool, Jud!"

"Will you put them down?"

"You want me to put them down?" I wondered, surprised that he was done playing.

"Yes, please."

"Okay, Jud. I'm also going to lay you back down and try to put you in a comfortable position." I was desperate for sleep but also somewhat sad that our time of playing inside Jud's head was over.

Until God heals my little Jud Bud, his speech is losing clarity so rapidly that I don't know how many more moments of precious communication I will have with him before he is completely mute.

After getting him settled, I encouraged him to talk to Jesus if he continued to have trouble sleeping. "Ask him to heal your body so that you can roll over again." I concluded by proclaiming, "Jesus loves you, Judson, even more than I do."

Upon hearing my declaration, Judson started to sing a song. I leaned in, trying to surmise what melody and lyrics were flowing from his lips.

"Jesus, name above all names. Beautiful Savior. Glorious Lord ... "[19]

My heart sang with him.

Letter 35: Sunday, September 16

Dear family and friends,

Drake is going to be taking a trip with Jud this week. My parents have some friends who live up north and are involved in a ministry of praying for the sick. They have worked things out for Drake and Jud to visit so that Jud can be soaked in prayer three hours a day, Monday through Thursday, surrounded by several people from churches all over the area, all of them being people who are committed to praying for the sick on a regular basis.

A trip like this presents many challenges considering Jud's current condition, but we want to be faithful to partner with those whom God has brought into our path on this journey.

We would covet your prayers as Drake and Jud make this trip. Please pray for safe travels. Please pray for Drake and Jud to have sweet father/son bonding time. Please pray for Jud to be comfortable and content. Please pray that he sleeps well. Please pray for Drake to have an extra measure of patience. Please pray for me; it is very difficult, on so many levels, to have them go and I am especially afraid Jud will not be able to talk when they return. Most of all, please pray for God to use these faithful people to touch our precious boy!

Thank you for partnering with us in prayer,
Christina (on behalf of Drake too)

Journal Entry: Sunday, September 16

Raw Moments

Drake and I had the chance to get a much-needed break from the kids today. My parents came over to our place this afternoon to watch Jud and Jessie, while we enjoyed dinner and a movie. Part of the movie depicted the loss of a loved one—it affected me significantly.

As we were driving home in the car, I burst into tears. It was an uncontrollable weeping that overtook my entire body. My hands even became numb.

"I'm afraid!" I gushed. "I'm afraid that you are going to return from your trip with Jud this week, and he will no longer be able to talk. I don't want to miss out on any of his words, and I can't bear to see him completely lose his ability to communicate." My sobbing made it difficult to speak. "I'm also afraid that I've believed God. I've believed God will heal Jud, and he might still die. I'm afraid. I am gravely afraid. I feel so vulnerable. I am scared."

I just kept crying out my fears. Drake listened.

My faith for Jud's healing is usually steadfast, but there are also very raw moments of fear, especially when I consider how this disease is destroying Judson's body, and I contemplate the magnitude of what I am actually asking God to do—I am overcome with doubt.

What if it turns out that his plans are not to heal Judson here on earth? Have we heard God incorrectly? Have we misunderstood his Word? Does he actually still heal supernaturally today? The questions flood my mind.

After several minutes of bawling and also trying to express my struggles, I started to calm.

Then Drake shared, "I'm afraid too."

We sat in silence. Our own thoughts bounced around in our heads for a while as the windows on the car steamed up.

Drake broke the silence. "Let's trust," he concluded, knowing the weight of risk that was wrapped up in his suggestion.

His words settled favorably in my heart. So in the steam on the windshield, I spelled it out with my index finger T-R-U-S-T.

Despite my fears, doubts, and the vulnerability of belief, trusting God sits well with my soul.

Letter 36: Wednesday, September 19

Dear family and friends,

As stated previously, Drake and Jud are up north, but Steve, a friend from church, opted to join Drake at the last minute. He has been an *incredible* blessing! Not only has he been an extra set of hands to help care for Jud (he even stayed up with Jud half the night last night), but he has also offered Drake significant friendship and support this week. We are *so* grateful for Steve and his family!

Drake has shared with me that Jud has had his ups and downs on the trip. Some evenings he has slept really well, and others have been rough. Fortunately, his disposition has been quite good, especially considering the fact that so many people have been praying for him, touching him, etc., for more than three hours a day. Jud has also had a voracious appetite, which is always good.

Drake mentioned over the phone how touched he has been by the outpouring of love he has received from the people he is with who are praying for Jud. He says they have been truly ministering to him and it has been a "sweet time." These new friends have tremendous faith to see God miraculously heal our son, and it is a great encouragement to us!

We continue to press in and beseech God to re-knit our precious boy's body!

All of your prayers are the most incredible gift we could possibly receive during this time! My friend Mary Phillips e-mailed me this word-image and it has stuck with me:

> Sometimes I imagine every prayer lifted for you by people from all over the world, some from friends, some from strangers. And what if every prayer fell in and on and around your home like a cotton ball, one cotton ball for each prayer? I do believe that most of the state and miles of the sea would be covered in several feet of pure, soft, white warmth. (This little image, now that I see it in writing, equates prayer with fluff… not my intention.) I wish you could literally be softly touched as you're prayed for and see an actual evidence of the cries to the Lord, especially in the quiet, dark, scary, overwhelming moments.

We are definitely feeling all your prayers. Thank you!

Much love and gratitude,
Christina (on behalf of Drake too)

Journal Entry: Wednesday, September 19

Awaken

There have been many times throughout the last couple months where it has felt like God is sleeping through our storm. Much like the story of Jesus and his disciples in Mark 4:35–41, life has brought a fierce wind along our journey, causing powerful waves to almost capsize our boat, and Jesus is in the stern, but it feels like he is asleep. I have often cried out to him, saying, "Do you not care that we are perishing?" (verse 38, NKJV).

However, I am realizing that it is not I who needs to awaken him, but rather he who wants to awaken me.

This journey of pain, our fierce storm, is intended to arouse me out of my slumber of mediocre, status-quo faith. When the time comes for God to rebuke the wind and the sea, whereby we find calm, it would be devastating to hear him say, "How is it that you have no faith?" (verse 40, NKJV).

Pain is a catalyst by which God wants to stimulate our faith. Oh that I might submit to that which he desires to awaken in me through this storm.

Journal Entry: Thursday, September 20

Needy

In one of the courses I taught to freshman college students, we would discuss the importance of community and particularly the value of interdependence. Yet, though I espoused these ideals, I knew I lived my own life giving greater value to independence; I was particularly afraid of being needy.

This trial has stripped me of many things but specifically my independent pride. I am desperately needy.

I was recently struck by the realization that every minute of every day I now need someone to be an extra set of hands so that both of my kids can be cared for. I am totally and completely incapable of taking care of Jud and Jessie by myself. I have also been inept at keeping our home in order, so others have taken up the slack to maintain the upkeep. Furthermore, my family would probably be foraging for food every night if not for the consistent meals we have received three times a week for the last couple months.

People have poured out their love on us, and we have needed it; I am dependent.

Maybe after my swing from independence to dependence, I will find the important balance of interdependence.

Letter 37: Friday, September 21

Dear family and friends,

Jud is still communicating! I know many of you were praying specifically for Jud's speech while Drake and Jud were on their trip; I was very thankful when they returned home today to find Jud was still talking. It is hard to understand him, but we can still make out some of what he is trying to say.

Thank you for your prayers,
Christina (on behalf of Drake too)

Saturday, September 22

Letter **by Drake Levasheff**

Dear family and friends,

However long it takes us to see Judson healed, I will always view this last week in Santa Maria as an important point on our journey. For each of our days there (Monday through Thursday), Jud was soaked in prayer for more than three hours by people who are committed intercessors for the sick. They have seen God heal cancer, diabetes, blindness, cystic fibrosis, and many other diseases.

It was a blessing seeing the Spirit of Jesus at work as they laid their hands on Jud and prayed with faith—we know that God hears such prayers. But more than that, we experienced the presence and peace of God and left with an abiding sense that God's Spirit is working to bring his full and complete healing to Jud here on earth. I've had faith to see Jud healed up until now, but what I have recently seen has bolstered my faith to an even greater degree.

Thank you for your support,
Drake

Journal Entry: Saturday, September 22

Hunker Down

Jessie had a sleepover with my parents last night, and Drake went to work early today, so Jud and I were alone this morning.

I couldn't bear it.

The destruction of this disease on Judson's body is so severe that it causes me to crumble when I have to sit alone in it for any chunk of time.

I find myself saying again and again behind tears, "I can't bear this! I can't bear this! I can't bear this!"

But I have to.

I want an option, but there is no option. I want to escape, but there is no escape. I want an easy answer, but there is no easy answer. I just have to keep sitting in it.

Oh God, please give me your peace as I hunker down.

Journal Entry: Sunday, September 23

Grasp the Rope Boldly

> Prayer is like a rope on a bell. When tugged, the great bell rings in the ears of God. Some scarcely stir the bell, for they pray so languidly; others give but an occasional pinch at the rope. But he who wins with heaven is the man who grasps the rope boldly and pulls continually with all his might.
>
> *Charles Spurgeon*[20]

I have been learning so much about prayer through this season; Drake, in particular, has been an incredible model of persistent prayer.

I am regularly discouraged and find it difficult to pray in my brokenness. There are also moments I give up hope, so I tend not to want to pray in my hopelessness either.

We are called to persistent prayer.

In reading Spurgeon, I am learning that persistence in prayer requires us to pursue it with an energy that never tires. When discouraged, we must increase our earnestness in asking. Even in hopelessness, persistence requires pleading with God until prayer prevails. By waiting patiently and praying persistently, we learn to trust God, we find strength under strain, and it develops a spirit of expectancy.

Drake is truly standing in the gap for his son. God has moved him to persistent prayer, and in Drake's persistence, I believe God is moved.

I am moved as well.

Journal Entry: Tuesday, September 25

Empty Vessel

This afternoon I was chatting in our office with my mom, who was holding Jud, and my dad, who was sitting at the computer. Meanwhile, Jessie meandered around the room enjoying her mobility and independence. All of sudden, Jessie tripped. As she fell, she banged her head on the corner of our desk. She hit it hard, with a sound that made us all cringe. Screams of pain erupted immediately, as did the indentation on her forehead. I jumped up, hoisted her into my embrace, and held her tightly as I tried to console her.

As she bawled, I began to weep too. Upon hearing my lament, my mom began to cry as well. It was a chorus of sobs.

I immediately recognized that I was not crying because Jessie was hurt (neither was my mom); my tears flowed because I have no reserves. I have no reserves for coping with even the smallest of challenges.

I am empty.

I am physically drained and depleted as Jud's needs continue to intensify. I am emotionally taxed as the deterioration of his body torments me. I am spiritually exhausted as my soul continues to be significantly stretched through this process.

I am weak. I am empty.

However, is it not an empty vessel that God can fill?

Fill me with your power, oh Lord, that my every breath may be a testimony of your strength being perfected in weakness.

Letter 38: Wednesday, September 26

Dear family and friends,

In many ways, Judson's needs are now like those of a new-born baby, only with greater frustration and intensity. He has tremendous difficulty expressing his needs, except through screams and cries. He must be carried everywhere (his legs and arms no longer work), and he does not have the muscle control to even hold up his head. Feeding is quite an under-taking, as we make every effort to get him to eat and drink (he has no means of feeding himself, and we even use an eye-dropper to get liquid in him).

He wakes frequently at night, needing care. He cannot be bathed without someone holding him in the bath. Though having been somewhat potty trained, he has lost control of his bowels and relies completely on diapers again (and it is very painful for him to move his legs in such a way that his diaper can be changed). On top of all that, it is hard to imag-ine that he is dealing with blindness too! Jud is now utterly and completely dependent, but what is even more difficult is that he has the knowledge that he has lost his independence (his mind remains sharp).

Because Jud requires constant care, every moment of every day necessitates one-on-one attention. Even when he sleeps, someone must tend to him. Because of Judson's increasing needs, starting Friday, our friend Melissa, who has worked with Jud in the nursery at church, will now be helping us in the afternoons when Sarah is unavailable.

Furthermore, my sister-in-law, Danielle, is looking into pro-viding a night aide so that Drake and I can consistently get a good night's sleep.

God is truly lavishing his love on us by the love of so many people. Thank you for walking alongside us in this journey!

Though I described the difficulty with all of Jud's symptoms, we continue to wait on God for his miraculous healing. Thank you to all who are standing with us in faith! I also think it is important to note that many of us who are around him regularly feel like we have not seen as rapid a progression of the disease in the last two weeks. We are thankful.

Admittedly, we are drained. I am still finding it very difficult to correspond with people individually. Thank you for continuing to write to us despite my lack of response and for extending us so much grace. Your words uplift us!

Much love and gratitude,
Christina (on behalf of Drake too)

Journal Entry: Wednesday, September 26

Rise Up and Walk

> In the name of Jesus Christ of Nazareth—rise up and walk!
>
> *Acts* 3:6 NKJV

Peter, under the power of the Holy Spirit, the same Spirit that resides in us as believers today, seized a lame man by his right hand and raised him up. Immediately the man's feet and ankles were strengthened. And with a leap, he stood upright and began to walk (Acts 3:7–8).

It is Jesus who healed this congenitally lame man. Jesus is the same now, and his power just as mighty as when he established his church in the book of Acts and exercised his authority through this healing.

We, the American church, talk about the power of the risen Lord without ever having really experienced it. What would it mean to truly taste and see the wonder and amazement of God's miraculous omnipotence?

Lives would be changed.

Lives would be changed, just as lives were changed by the Prince of Life in Acts 3. I imagine Judson "walking, leaping, and praising God," wherein all who see, marvel at the power of Jesus. Let it be on the basis of faith in his name, the name of Jesus, that our boy who we see and know be strengthened, and may the faith that comes through him give Jud perfect health in the presence of us all (Acts 3:16).

In the name of Jesus Christ of Nazareth—rise up and walk, Judson!

Journal Entry: Sunday, September 30

Blind

It is not uncommon when Jud is crying out during his naps or the middle of the night for me to go and lay my head next to his, face-to-face. The other day I had my face just inches away from Jud's after giving him a big kiss. I was lying there watching him; we were not exchanging words.

Suddenly he got this very fearful look on his face and began to cry. Though his eyes were looking directly at me, he had no idea I was right there in front of him; he thought I had left the room. He felt alone. He was scared. He felt vulnerable.

Blind.

Jud was blind to my presence, and in that moment, I began to wonder whether or not I am often blind to God's presence. Are there times when Jesus is directly in front of me, only "inches" away, and yet I think he's elsewhere? When I feel alone, are we actually face-to-face? When I feel scared, is he actually there trying to comfort me? When I feel vulnerable, am I unaware that I am under his perfect protection?

Am I spiritually blind?

I placed my hand on Jud's back and gently patted him; he immediately calmed and then smiled. He was reassured of my presence, and his fears abated.

I feel alone. I am scared. I feel vulnerable.

Jesus, will you gently pat my back so I know you're there? I don't always have eyes that see you.

Letter 39: Tuesday, October 2

Dear family and friends,

On Sunday a gentleman at church asked me how much longer we think Jud has before he dies. He was the first person who has ever boldly asked me this question. As I responded, I realized there are probably many others who are wondering the same thing but have not asked.

God has given us *many* reasons to believe he intends to heal Jud, so we wait expectantly for his deliverance. That being said, the situation in Judson's body is becoming dire and could likely lead to death before year's end, apart from divine intervention. The doctors look at the rate of progression of the disease thus far to provide an approximation as to how much longer his body may be able to survive.

It has been less than four months since the onset of Krabbe and, as you know, Jud has already lost all capability in his neck and body, he is blind, he is nearly mute, and he is having difficulty with his bowels. Were the progression of the disease to continue at the same rate (though it appears to have possibly slowed a bit the last couple weeks), we would be shocked for his body to survive more than two more months (a liberal estimate) if not healed by the touch of Almighty God. Our research indicates that, unabated, Krabbe could soon begin attacking critical functions of the body; the ability to swallow would probably be the next thing to deteriorate. This leads to loss of appetite, and other systems in the body shut down soon thereafter.

As of today, Jud is still eating pretty well and swallowing even thin liquids (the hardest to consume) without too much difficulty—he chokes periodically. His hearing remains intact. He still smiles (the most beautiful smile one could ever imagine!) in response to people and ideas, tries to give kisses, makes efforts to express his thoughts through garbled words, enjoys going for a stroll, likes to pretend to walk, finds great pleasure in listening to stories, and loves to have people stimulate his imagination.

The daily care for Jud is taxing beyond words, but … Judson is *such* a tremendous blessing and joy! We continue to thank God for our little gift and feel honored that the Lord saw fit to entrust him to our care!

Much love,
Christina (on behalf of Drake too)

Letter 40: Sunday, October 7

Dear family and friends,

A doctor, one of the leading researchers for newborn screening of Krabbe disease in New York, contacted us. She indicated that Jud's situation throws a wrench into some of their assumptions about Krabbe thus far. As I've stated previously, the onset of Krabbe symptoms typically occurs in infancy (90 percent). Jud had late-infantile/juvenile onset (less than 10 percent). Children with late onset usually experience a *much* slower progression of the disease, which enables opportunities for stem cell transplants, etc. However, in Jud's case, though onset of symptoms was late, the progression of symptoms has been extremely rapid. The doctor indicated that this is somewhat unfamiliar territory in their research. In fact, she asked for us to send pictures and other information so that she can use Jud as an example of a divergent case.

How much more of an example of a "divergent case" would he be if touched by the miraculous healing power of Almighty God! We keep praying to that end!

We remain amazed by the outpouring of support we are receiving. Thank you to all who continue to hold us up in prayer, whether through a scheduled time slot or just generally as God brings us to mind. We are absolutely touched at how God has captured the hearts and attention of so many and focused them on our little family in our time of need. How good he truly is!

Thank you to those who have noticed that I have not been writing as much in the last couple weeks. I am truly amazed that people care. As Jud's needs increase, my pockets of time for writing are diminishing. Furthermore, when I do get a moment, I haven't had the energy necessary for putting my thoughts on paper. Though I haven't been writing as much, God continues to stretch my faith in some incredible ways. I am grateful and hope to write about some of my experiences soon.

Much love and gratitude,
Christina (on behalf of Drake too)

Journal Entry: Monday, October 8

Breath of Life

An unfamiliar passage in the Old Testament (2 Kings 4:8–36) was brought to my attention by my friend Tamie. Upon reading it, I felt a strong kinship with the woman in the story.

There was a Shunammite woman who tended to the needs of Elisha, a holy man of God. Later, Elisha learned that this woman had no son. So he called to her and prophesied, "About this time next year, you will hold a son in your arms."

"No, my lord," she objected. "Don't mislead your servant, O man of God!" (2 Kings 4:15)

But the woman became pregnant, and the next year, about the same time, she gave birth to a son, just as Elisha had told her.

Similarly, I had not asked God for a child; rather, I had resigned myself to the fact that I was probably barren. The Lord shocked us with my first pregnancy and the gift of our precious Jud (see previous journal entry on July 27, 2007: Perfect Gift).

The Shunammite woman's child grew and one day complained to his father of pain in his head. He was carried to his mother, sat on her lap until noon, and then the boy died.

The woman set out to find Elisha, and when she reached

the man of God, she took hold of his feet and said, "Did I ask you for a son, my lord? Didn't I tell you, 'Don't raise my hopes'?" (2 Kings 4:28).

Correspondingly, I have wondered, "Father, you have given me Jud, a gift I didn't even request from you, and from the time he was in my womb I asked you to guard and protect his life. Do you really intend to take him away so quickly?"

Elisha went to the woman's house and found the boy lying dead on the couch. He prayed to the Lord, lay upon the child, and revived him!

The woman came in and fell at his feet and bowed to the ground. Then she took her son and went out.

Oh, that this reviving breath of life from the Lord touch our Jud too! And may many, along with us, fall at Jesus' feet, bowing in worship!

Letter 41 : Tuesday, October 9

Dear family and friends,

It feels like everything has intensified with Jud over the last couple days. We have observed that his ability to deal with the affects of Krabbe has diminished significantly; he is uncomfortable, and his pain, frustration, and sleep difficulties have increased exponentially, rather than the usual periodic waves. It is almost as though the disease was in a holding pattern for a couple weeks and now it has kicked into high gear again.

In light of this, it became clearly evident that it was time to start giving him the prescribed sedative. Prior to this week, we had not given him any drugs; previously it felt like the choice to administer drugs to Jud would have been more for our benefit, to mellow him so we could cope; but it is now obvious that Jud needs the drugs so that he can cope. Furthermore, we had not wanted to lose any of Jud's lucid moments, but our choice to give him the drug now is enabling him the opportunity to regain some mellow moments of smiles and even laughter. Seeing as this is an issue we have been grappling with for quite some time, I am so thankful that God made it clearly evident that this was the next best step.

Our current attention is focused on Jud's mouth and his ability to swallow. It became apparent on Sunday that he is no longer able to chew his food; we are giving him soft, blended, or finely chopped foods now. His appetite varies from meal to meal.

Jud is often in pain when he has a big yawn because his jaw is tightening just like the joints in the rest of his body have already experienced. We are also starting to hear the beginning signs of mucous in his throat—the doctor said this occurs when the saliva/mucous that the body naturally produces cannot be swallowed in the throat. As this increases, it will create a rattling sound with each breath.

I would describe our recent circumstances as having turned another dark corner in this journey, but we continue to await Jud's deliverance. Right now we would covet your prayers for increased faith, courage, strength, endurance, and trust. We also desperately need wisdom!

God is good. Though there are times in the last couple months where I have felt unheard by him, I can point to far more instances that reflect his love and grace toward us. God is definitely good! Please continue to join us in praising him for the precious little boy he has given us, the way he is working in this situation, and the undying love he pours out on his children.

Much love and gratitude,
Christina (on behalf of Drake too)

Journal Entry: Tuesday, October 9

Death has been Conquered

Jesus Christ conquered death. Therefore, Krabbe, this heinous disease, can hold no power over our family; it was defeated on the cross. Krabbe cannot claim victory over Jud's life, whether or not Jud's mortal body has breath (and we continue to await God's healing touch that extends Jud's years of breath) because Jesus offers life—eternal life!

In all our pain and uncertainty, I embrace the life-giving hope found in Jesus Christ!

Letter 42: Friday, October 12

Dear family and friends,

As stated in my last letter, the severity of Jud's condition has increased dramatically in the last week. The situation in his body is dire. As his ability to swallow is diminishing, his appetite has waned. He is now on a sedative 'round the clock. However, I would definitely not describe him as listless. He's still our brave little fighter with smiles that run from ear to ear many times throughout the day! He communicates "yes" or "no" to us by moving his tongue and continues to be quite aware of his surroundings; his mind and ability to hear are certainly functioning well. I can't imagine all the thoughts running around in his head, but I pray he has an overwhelming sense of our love and especially God's love for him!

Our strength and peace are rising as we wait upon the Lord.

We have decided to open our home for an *open house* this weekend. We realize there may be people during this season who want to come over and see us or Jud, but an opportunity has not been available. We welcome *anyone*—people we know, people we don't know, people who have already been to our home, people who have not, those who want to see Jud, sing to him, pray for him, or just love him in person. So if you feel so led, please feel free to come by.

Much love,
Christina (on behalf of Drake too)

Journal Entry: Friday, October 12

The Delicate Balance

I have found this trial to be a delicate balance.

On one hand, we have been allowing God to foster in us an unwavering faith for Judson's healing, clinging to the promises of the Word, knowing we serve a Father who is rich in mercy and compassion and quick to answer his children. We continue to wait expectantly!

Yet we are also surrendering completely to the sovereign hand of the Almighty, recognizing his ways are perfect and his love boundless. We yield to the work he wants to do in and through this suffering.

As we raise Judson into the arms of Jesus, we release him, knowing the Lamb of God who conquered death may give Jud back to us for more years on earth or choose to keep our precious little man in his loving embrace. Either outcome brings deliverance for Jud and praise from our lips!

Month Five:
Surrendering in Heartache

Letter 43: Sunday, October 14

Dear family and friends,

We had our open house this evening, and it was wonderful! We were shocked to have over 120 people drop in during our last-minute open house—people who live locally, and people who drove from as far as Arizona. People we know and see on a regular basis, people from our past, and people we had never met before blessed us with their presence.

Our intent was to give others an opportunity to see Jud, but we were *tremendously* blessed in the process.

Much love and gratitude,
Christina (on behalf of Drake too)

Journal Entry: Sunday, October 14

Real

God poured out his love on us significantly tonight—through people.

We were blessed by faces we see regularly, faces from the past, and even faces we've never met before—faces of faith, hope, and love!

It is incredible. It is humbling. It is staggering. It is rich. It is moving. It is encouraging. It is grace.

I will hold in my heart the embraces, the tears, the special care for our boy, the prayers, the songs, the personal reflections, the calls, the gifts, and so much more.

This evening was a powerful glimpse of the love we have

been receiving for several months, a love that points to our Father.

This love is real. He is real.

Letter 44: Thursday, October 18

Dear family and friends,

Krabbe continues to take its toll on Jud's body. His appetite is lessening, and his ability to swallow diminishing. I am desperate for him to communicate with me and miss his voice so much! I can't even begin to describe how difficult it is to watch him suffer. This is excruciating! However, we continue to fight the spiritual battle for Judson's life and pray that God is being glorified as we beseech him for Jud's healing here on earth.

Thank you for caring,
Christina (on behalf of Drake too)

Journal Entry: Thursday, October 18

A Ready Smile

I have so much to learn from my little man.

In the midst of such tremendous suffering, in between moans of pain or screams from being uncomfortable, Judson has a ready smile; he smiles frequently, even if he was just crying the moment before. It is so incredibly beautiful that my heart almost bursts every time I see him beam!

Here is a boy who has lost almost everything, and yet his countenance is regularly one of genuine joy.

In my season of suffering, I long to have this kind of joy permeate my soul, to learn to walk fully in my pain while embracing the wonder offered with each breath.

Teach me, Judson. Teach me.

Letter 45: Friday, October 19

Dear family and friends,

Judson is having difficulty swallowing his own saliva now—choking and gagging can occur. Therefore, hospice provided us with a suction machine today to help dry up his mouth. Furthermore, though he is on a sedative (and the dose was doubled a day ago) he has been having many more moments where he just seems to be miserable. We are praying for wisdom as to the next steps for making him comfortable.

On the flipside, he is still able to eat some foods of a certain consistency, and he consumed a decent amount of food today. We are watching his appetite very closely, seeing as it is a significant indicator as to whether his body is shutting down.

The situation in Jud's body is grave, but God's ability to heal him is no different today than it was the day he was diagnosed with Krabbe disease. We continue to be relentless in our pursuit of God through this circumstance and our pleading with him to rain down his kingdom power in Judson's body. Thank you to all who are laboring with us in prayer—let us not lose heart!

Much love and gratitude,
Christina (on behalf of Drake too)

Journal Entry: Saturday, October 20

The Huge Arrow

I must confess that there are moments I get so caught up in my desire to see Judson healed that I miss the huge arrow formed in this suffering, the arrow that is intended to point me toward deeper intimacy with my heavenly Father. This circumstance of pain is intended to catapult me into his arms; am I sitting in his embrace?

The other day, our new friend Rebekah reminded me of the passage of Scripture in Luke 5:17–26, where some friends lowered a paralytic man through the roof of a home so that Jesus could see him and heal him. He told the man that his sins were forgiven. The Pharisees questioned Jesus' ability to forgive sins. His response to the Pharisees was, "Which is easier; to say, 'Your sins are forgiven,' or to say, 'Get up and walk'?" (verse 23). He then healed the lame man.

When I pondered this passage, I was struck by how much easier it was for Jesus to heal a man's broken body than for him to forgive sins; this encouraged me to consider the simplicity by which Jesus can heal Jud.

However, as I continued to ponder this passage, I realized that I was so wrapped up in my desire to see God stretch out his healing hand to touch Jud that I was brushing by the actual point of the passage. Jesus' ability to heal a broken body is nothing compared to the gravity of Jesus forgiving my sins.

I have been healed! I have been set free from the bondages of sin. I have been redeemed out of my brokenness. I have been called into communion with the God of the universe. My transgressions have been covered by the blood of Jesus. I have been touched by the Lord of all creation and made whole.

This is where the story is. This is where we find hope. And it is out of this realization that I want to live.

How amazing that Jesus has invited me to sit in his embrace, to feel his loving arms around me, to bask in his love.

I have been healed!

Journal Entry: Sunday, October 21

First Thing

I am fairly confident that Jesus will be the first thing Jud sees when he is set free from the afflictions of Krabbe.

Whether Jesus visits Jud here on earth and heals his body so he can have more years of life or whether Jud meets Jesus in heaven, I am convinced that Judson is going to see Jesus soon. I sense that the type of miraculous work required for Jud's healing can only come from being in the powerful presence of Jesus Christ himself.

And so we talk about it with Jud.

I tell Jud how Jesus is going to kiss him and love on him and how he is going to heal his body soon so that he can run and walk and see and talk again. I tell Jud how much Jesus loves him and cares for him, particularly in all his suffering.

Last night, as we were discussing this, I said to Jud, "Hey, let's think of a song you can sing to Jesus when you see him."

The biggest and brightest smile overtook his face. He loved the idea!

So we sang different songs. Each time, we asked Jud if the song we had just sung was the song he wanted to sing to Jesus when he sees him. This is the song that seemed to emerge as the front-runner:

Arms of Love[21]

I sing a simple song of love
To my Savior, to my Jesus
I'm grateful for the things you've done
My loving Savior, my precious Jesus

My heart is glad that you've called me your
own
And there's no place I'd rather be

Than in your arms, arms of love
In your arms, arms of love
Holding me still
Holding me near
In your arms of love

Letter 46: Tuesday, October 23

Dear family and friends,

Jessie and I woke up sick this morning. This is particularly problematic for Jud; the doctor indicated that any type of illness would increase the progression of the disease dramatically. The two of us are keeping our distance from Jud, but we would appreciate your prayers for him to stay healthy.

Our last update came on the heels of a rough week, but Jud has been doing so much better these last four days. He has been eating very well, we haven't needed to use the suction machine, and his disposition has been wonderful (without any change in medication). He has been full of life—smiles, laughter, and general contentment. We are *very* thankful!

Much love and gratitude,
Christina (on behalf of Drake too)

Letter 47: Thursday, October 25

Dear family and friends,

Jud's hospice nurse comes to visit once a week, usually on

Thursday mornings. Last week, the situation was pretty dismal. I remember asking her what we should expect to see next, and she hesitated to answer my question but rather gave me a knowing look as if to indicate she didn't expect Jud would last much longer.

This morning when the same nurse came, she exclaimed, "Oh my goodness, Jud seems to be doing *so* much better. His disposition is better, his muscle tone is better, and he's eating and swallowing better. Wow!" She kept repeating her excitement over how much better Jud was doing. She mentioned that even if we had increased his drugs, it couldn't account for what she was seeing (and we haven't increased his drugs). Later, with tears almost filling her eyes, she asked, "What have you been doing?"

I responded, "Praying. We've been praying."

The nurse wrote on Jud's weekly progress report that he has "stabilized."

We serve a God who cannot only stabilize our son from imminent death but can completely restore his body back to wholeness. We are encouraged and hopeful; we hope *all* who are praying for us will be encouraged as well.

May our strength, faith, and hope continue to rise as we wait upon the Lord!

Jessie and I are still sick and having to keep our distance from Jud. We continue to pray his protection from illness. Other than a sneeze here or there, Jud hasn't shown any signs of picking up the virus from us.

Along those lines, I hope to heal soon. It has been so hard not to be able to kiss and love on Jud these last couple days!

With love and hope,
Christina (on behalf of Drake too)

Journal Entry: Friday, October 26

Believing Otherwise

I remember the day so vividly...

We were sitting in a conference room at the Kaiser Sunset Metabolic Clinic in Los Angeles. Three doctors sat around the table with us: the geneticist, neurologist, and metabolosist, along with a couple nurses. They were using an overhead projector to go over the information obtained from Jud's MRI and MRSpectroscopy.

The doctors talked amongst themselves while they also went over the results with us. As I was looking at the information on the screen and straining to hear every word the doctors spoke, my eyes landed on the term "leukodystrophy." Suddenly all the blood in my head seemed to race to my heart.

I had actually gone into this meeting thinking, "Please do not let me hear the word leukodystrophy." I had done enough online research to know that any type of leukodystrophy was severe, incurable, and ultimately fatal. Yet based on Jud's symptoms, I also knew in my heart that it was a real possibility.

So there I was, sitting in this sterile room, Drake next to me, Jud sitting on his lap playing with a car, frozen in extreme shock and pain. Then the geneticist said it: "We believe your son has a form of leukodystrophy. We don't know what kind of leukodystrophy (there are dozens), but he will not get better. Things are only going to get worse. We are going to do a spinal tap right now, but you need to know this is very severe. This is not going to get better. This can only get worse. Until we know which leukodystrophy, we do not have details for you, but this is not going to get better. This is not going away, and it will progressively get worse."

The doctor must have told us that the disease "would not get better" about six or seven times; she made sure we knew further deterioration was the only path for Jud.

Since that day, the Lord has been developing a faith in us to believe otherwise.

The next time we met with the geneticist and neurologist, they explained that Judson had Krabbe disease. At the end of our meeting with them, Drake expressed gratitude for all their efforts on our behalf and then plainly stated, "We believe in the Lord Jesus Christ who can heal anything. This disease is certainly not beyond him. We will wait expectantly!"

And so we have and will continue to do so.

Journal Entry: Saturday, October 27

Deep, Lasting Mark

I never imagined my life with this kind of pain, the kind of pain that follows you every moment, every day, month after month, without an ending in sight; the kind of pain that causes your life as you once knew it to cease altogether; the kind of pain that leaves you waking up every morning trying to figure out how to manage each moment so you can make it through the day, only to go through it all again the next day.

This is a pain you cannot escape even when you have opportunities to "get away"; a pain that redefines how people perceive you; and a pain that filters into all your conversations, creative expressions, and most minute thoughts. It is an internal pain that causes physical responses in your body. This kind of pain leaves you longing for normalcy when you are in a sea of people whose lives seem to carry on as usual, and it reshapes every relationship in your life. I am describing a pain that will leave a deep, lasting mark on you forever.

It is not that I expected to be immune from pain. In fact, the day I found out I was first pregnant I knew I was suddenly vulnerable to new pains by becoming a parent. But in all honesty, I never expected this kind of pain, the type of pain I had watched in movies or read about in books and newspapers or heard about through word of mouth but never imagined I would actually experience myself.

I remember sitting in a Jana Alayra concert when Jud was less than a year old and hearing her tell the story of how she lost one of her daughters in a car accident. There was not a dry eye in the room as she shared her pain and suffering with us. However, as I cried with her, trying to imagine the incredible grief she experienced over the loss of her child, I admit I was brazen enough to think I would probably never face that type of pain. I was naïve.

Tragedy is more common than I thought.

The question is, in my life, what will be the deep, lasting mark left by this pain?

Letter 48: Sunday, October 28

Dear family and friends,

We are so grateful that Jud's condition continues to be very stable. Next, instead of seeing more deterioration again, we hope to see healing flood his body.

We serve a mighty God who is definitely moving and working in this situation. We will continue to keep our eyes on him!

Much love,
Christina (on behalf of Drake too)

Journal Entry: Sunday, October 28

Defying the Downward Spiral

Twelve days ago I was shopping at Trader Joes, and while standing in the checkout line, a woman who lives near us was in line next to me. We started chatting, and she asked about Jud. I told her that his body was deteriorating rapidly. She had brought us a meal a couple weeks before and mentioned that she would love to bring us another meal in a couple months. I hesitated, then expressed what was really on my heart: "I don't think we'll need meals that far out."

"What do you mean?" she inquired.

"The situation in Jud's body is dire. He can hardly swallow anymore."

With great care she followed up with another question: "How much longer do you think he has?"

"Well, we are still praying with expectation that God will heal him, but outside of his touch, I would guess that Jud's body cannot hold out much longer than two weeks. And that might be a liberal estimate."

Today is Sunday, and this Tuesday will mark two weeks since that conversation.

Jud's health has definitely improved. I am no longer concerned that we are on the brink of his body shutting down. On Thursday the hospice nurse came to our home and exclaimed, "Jud is doing so much better!" We knew it and had observed it, but we were being cautious, not wanting to be overly optimistic with our observations. Hence, it was great to have a knowledgeable outsider observe Jud's improvement too.

Interestingly, the nature of all leukodystrophies is such that symptoms cannot improve. The myelin sheath, which protects the nerves and enables the brain to transmit messages to the rest of the body, is being destroyed. A child that is blind and lame because of a leukodystrophy has eyes and legs that work perfectly, but the brain is demyelinating, causing it to no longer be able to send and receive messages to and from those parts of the body; science and medicine have not yet discovered a way to remyelinate the brain. Therefore, as the myelin sheath deteriorates—in Krabbe disease, this is due to a deficiency in what is called the GALC enzyme—various capabilities are lost, never to be regained. It is a downward spiral.

Does Jud's recent improvement defy the downward spiral of a leukodystrophy? Once a capability is lost, it cannot be regained; it cannot get better … unless, of course, God is at work.

We have no idea what to expect tomorrow, but we certainly have reason to praise him today!

Letter 49: Monday, October 29

Dear family and friends,

I wrote last night how Judson was still very stable; however, when we woke this morning, the night aide informed us that Jud got a high fever in the middle of the night. His fever is still very high this morning. Furthermore, he does not want to drink or eat anything.

It appears he has caught the same illness that Jessie and I are still battling, along now with my mom, dad, and Melissa, who helps watch him in the afternoons (but because of the shared germs, I am grateful we will no longer have to keep our distance from him). As I stated in a previous update, it is very severe for Jud to get ill at this stage in the game, and it certainly heightens our concern.

We would covet your prayers for protection of Jud's body this morning and the next days to come.

Thank you for your love and support!

Much love,
Christina (on behalf of Drake too)

Letter 50: Tuesday, October 30

Dear family and friends,

Judson seems to be doing a little bit better today. Yesterday his fever was pretty high, he didn't eat a single thing, and it was hard to get him to consume liquids. This morning he ate one-third of a banana pureed, had some apple juice, and his fever has dropped a bit. He is not irritable but rather very lethargic (we're not sure whether this is good or bad). He is sleeping well, and we hope this helps his body mend quickly. Just like the rest of us who are sick, he has deep congestion, which could be most problematic.

We are so grateful for your prayers!

We continue to be showered with love and support, but I have been unable to keep up with our thank yous. Please know that our gratitude abounds for the numerous ways we are being loved. I only wish my words could reflect how our lives have been touched by kindness, generosity, thoughtfulness, service, and love. We consider ourselves considerably blessed! *Thank you!*

Along those lines, I cannot even begin to express our gratitude for the generous donations of *so* many that have made it possible for us to keep Judson at home during this season.

We now have caretakers throughout the day (weekdays) and a night aide who sleeps in Jud's room with him (five days a week). Thank you also to my dad, brother, and many people from our church who have filled in and cared for Jud on the nights that aren't covered by our night aide. It is important to note that our sanity level went up 100 percent when we started getting a full night's sleep again.

Much love and gratitude,
Christina (on behalf of Drake too)

Journal Entry: Tuesday, October 30

Too Much

> Most of my life I've made the mistake of believing God for too little. For the rest of my life, if I have to make a mistake, it's going to be believing God for too much. But how can you believe an omnipresent, omniscient, omnipotent God for too much, especially when he himself says, "Everything is possible for him who believes" (Mark 9:23).
>
> *Jack Deere*[22]

Oh Father, forgive me for limiting you. Please help me to see the truth of your presence and power. I want to hear you, above the clanging sounds of this world, even when your voice is still and small. Help me to approach your throne with expectation. Please grow my faith.

Letter 51: Thursday, November 1

Dear family and friends,

I told Drake that he should probably write this update because I might make things sound like we're in the abyss, but he encouraged me to write it anyway.

It has been a very rough week here at the Levasheff home. Jud has had a high fever pretty consistently, though it dropped a couple times. For the most part, he has had little to no appetite—he ate yesterday but has not wanted to eat anything today. We have to work very hard to get him to consume liquids. He is quite lethargic, fragile, and weak. We are very concerned about him.

Many of us are still fighting illness too. My mom, dad, Jessie, and I continue to battle significant colds. However, late last night I also got a tremendous headache with nausea and have been out of commission. Therefore, Jessie and I will be staying with my folks for the day, while Drake and our other caretakers look after Jud. Somehow, Drake has been able to avoid getting sick, but he has been carrying a heavier load because so many of us are sick. We pray Drake continues to stay well and maintain his strength. He's been amazing!

Call us crazy, but we got the kids dressed up for Halloween and went "trick-or-treating" to a couple homes last night. Jud was a racecar driver, and we took him around in his special seat. Unfortunately, after the novelty of being a racecar driver wore off, Jud didn't last very long. He had enjoyed "trick-or-treating" so much last year that he had asked me the next day if we could do it again. At that time, I told him he would have to wait another year. As with so much now, it was heart wrenching to see it hold nothing for him this time.

We are worn thin. We are weary.

We would covet your prayers for strength, healing of all our bodies, and, of course, complete restoration of Judson's frail frame.

As always, thank you for your love and support!

Much love,
Christina (on behalf of Drake too)

Letter 52: Saturday, November 3

Dear family and friends,

Judson is showing many signs indicative of one who is approaching the end of life. We would covet your prayers!

We stand in agreement with our loving heavenly Father's

perfect will for our beloved boy, and continue to ask him to heal his broken body.

Thank you for standing with us in faith, hope, and love! Christina and Drake

Letter 53: Sunday, November 4

Dear family and friends,

Big Jud is hanging in there. Drake and I had a "sleepover" with him in his room last night, and though it didn't offer us much rest, we had some very sweet times of holding him in our arms. He is certainly a fighter!

Based on the professional opinion of Drake's sister, Danielle, and her husband, Marty, who are both nurses, the situation in Jud's body is such that things could turn at any moment or stay as they are for even a couple days.

Right now Jud is still cognizant at times and even smiling periodically—particularly when his sister is present, hugging and kissing him. We continue to have many precious and sweet moments.

It is amazing and encouraging to see the faith of so many who have posted their love and support. Just as Jud is a fighter, we will continue to fight the battle of faith alongside him. We cherish the prayers of God's people offered across the world and those who want to pray for Jud in our home. Our boy is in the arms of a loving, merciful, and powerful God!

Your words have been a constant source of hope and love; they are a reminder that we are definitely not walking alone. Thank you!

Much love,
Christina and Drake

Letter 54: Monday, November 5

Dear family and friends,

Our day has been filled with numerous tears but also some smiles. It became very apparent that Jud's pain was increasing exponentially, and it was time to give him morphine. When we first administered the morphine, a peace swept over his face, and he was once again responding to our conversations with beautiful smiles. It was a sweet time. He slowly drifted off to sleep. However, his sleep has gotten deeper and deeper, even though we haven't given him any more of the painkiller. I would describe him as being in a semi-comatose, if not fully comatose, state.

We have been advised by the doctor not to force him to eat or drink at this stage. *Yikes!*

Our hearts are filled with numerous emotions, too many to describe here, but as I stated in a previous post a few weeks ago, we believe God is just as able to heal Jud today as he was the day we discovered that Jud had Krabbe disease. We are convinced that our Father is doing something incredible for his glory through this journey—evidenced even today by the amazing words of faith offered to us by so many of you.

The Lord has poured out his peace upon us, and we continue to trust him. We have much to be thankful for—gratitude is being impressed upon our hearts.

> Praise the Lord, O my soul; all my inmost being, praise his holy name. Praise the Lord, O my soul, and forget not all his benefits— who forgives all your sins and heals all your diseases, who redeems your life from the pit and crowns you with love and compassion, who satisfies your desires with good things so that your youth is renewed like the eagle's.
>
> *Psalm* 103:1–5

We are upheld by your prayers as we walk the unknown path already laid out before us.

In his grip,
Christina and Drake

Journal Entry: Monday, November 5

Alive

Tonight my beautiful boy lay in my lap like a rag doll, his body exhibiting signs of impending loss of life. His mouth was open, and his warm breath quietly hissed as it escaped his chest. It was just the two of us—breathing, resting, motionless. The clock on the wall ticked loudly, as if it was counting each moment while also giving rhythm to the silence of the night.

My mind was racing.

I began to ponder the mingling of beauty and suffering, evidenced in Judson's soft face.

Similarly, my soul is full of numerous intertwined emotions, many of which seem contradictory: joy and pain, strength and weakness, faith and fear, peace and unrest, hope and concern, wonder and confusion. The complexity of these emotions is indicative of being alive.

The complexity of beauty and suffering in Judson's body reminded me that he too is still very much alive!

Journal Entry: Tuesday, November 6

Dear Little Levy...

This is a letter I wrote to Judson while he was still being knit together in my womb. I hadn't planned to give it to him until he was much older, but I decided to read it to him today.

October 19, 2004

My Dear Little Levy,

You are already so precious to me, and I haven't even laid eyes on you yet. I feel you move in my belly, and my heart leaps—you bring life to my soul. I am in awe and honored that the Lord has chosen to knit you together in my womb. What a blessing and a gift!

Today marks exactly ten weeks from the day you are due. At times it seems like a long way off because I have such excitement and anticipation over your arrival. Other times it feels like your entry into this world is just moments away, and I don't necessarily feel prepared, but I still can't wait!

Your dad and I have been busy getting ready to bring you into our family. We have been preparing your nursery, buying various baby items, taking childbirth classes, and reading lots of books about pregnancy, delivery, and parenting. It is definitely a new world—from the lambs on our wall, to the onesies in our closet, to the infant car seat in our garage, we have already begun to enter parenthood.

Even more important than all the tangible preparations, I have been preparing my heart, mind, and soul. I feel a grave responsibility as a mother and often feel unworthy. You will quickly know how fragile, frail, and fallible I am. I entreat the Lord for his mercy and grace in my parenting, for I know I already fall short. I ask your forgiveness even now for all the ways my issues will adversely affect you or hurt you. I pray God will use me in your life as a reflection of his love, despite my shortcomings. He has entrusted your care to your dad and me—I am his tool, and I surrender myself to his will.

I pray for your soul. I long for you to grow with a heart that is oriented toward God. May your first and foremost goal be to glorify him and ultimately love the people around you. I hope you have sensitivity to his spirit at a young age, and when you fall short, as we all do, may you quickly run to the throne of your heavenly Father, allowing his cleansing grace to pour over you. He has promised to be your shepherd, and he longs for you to follow. Your dad and I long to teach you these principles, particularly by the way we live our lives, but we will fall short. Follow the Great Shepherd. Unlike your dad and me, he will not let you down.

You will be entering a tough world that does not want to acknowledge your Creator, but Christ has already defeated the enemy. As this culture wars for your soul, stand strong and maintain an eternal perspective, for the influences of this day are fleeting. Put your stock in that which moth and rust cannot destroy.

As I write this letter, you are moving in my tummy. I sit with wonder as to what you will look like and who you will become. Will you be a boy or a girl? Will you have a mellow personality like your dad or will you be a little more fiery like me? What will your interests be? Music? Athletics? Art? Who will your friends be? What influences will tempt you? What will bring tears in your life? What will bring laughter and smiles to your face? Your laugher will be music to my senses. I have tremendous hopes for you, and I cannot wait to hold you in my arms, look in your eyes, and kiss you to pieces. No trial or challenges can supersede the depths of my love for you. You are a precious gift! You are a joy!

I know not what tomorrow will bring, what heartache or sorrow, joy or triumph, but one thing is certain: you are deeply loved! You are

encircled by God's supernatural and uncondi-
tional love, and never ever forget how much
your dad and I love you too!

With all my heart,
Your mom

Letter 55: Tuesday, November 6

Dear family and friends,

We continue to be surrounded in love by family and friends,
both physically in our home and incredibly by the prayers,
thoughts, and faith of thousands around the globe. We are
grateful for the numerous ways we are being inundated with
care and compassion.

Our sweet Jud Bud is still fighting—fighting hard! Each
strained breath requires the strength of his entire body. He
is experiencing apnea, as his breathing patterns are irregular,
sometimes with several seconds in between breaths. His last
lucid moment was at 3:45 a.m. yesterday morning.

We feel like we have been called to walk this seemingly contradictory path of completely releasing our son into the arms
of the Giver of Life who loves Jud far more deeply than we
can imagine, while standing strong in faith for our Father's
deliverance by supernaturally healing Jud here on earth.

We trust. We trust in the goodness of God and expect Jud
will be touched by Jesus in one way or another very soon.

> Do you not know? Have you not heard? The
> Lord is the everlasting God, the Creator of
> the ends of the earth. He will not grow tired
> or weary, and his understanding no one can
> fathom. He gives strength to the weary and

increases the power of the weak. Even youths grow tired and weary, and young men stumble and fall; but those who hope in the Lord will renew their strength. They will soar on wings like eagles; they will run and not grow weary, they will walk and not be faint.

Isaiah 40:28–31

We have hope and we stand in hope tonight.

Much love,
Christina and Drake

Journal Entry: Tuesday, November 6

Lucid

It was the early hours of the morning on Monday when I had a "shift" alone with Jud. I had been singing and reading Scripture to him throughout the night, while also enjoying some moments of quiet. Jud was in a semi-comatose state and had been since 1:00 p.m. the afternoon prior.

Around 3:45 a.m., I came to the realization that I hadn't really been engaging Jud directly, though I was very present with him. So I decided to start singing songs that he enjoys. I began to sing "The Itsy Bitsy ~~Spider~~ Elephant"[23] and then proclaimed, as we often do, "That's too big!" All of a sudden, a huge smile emerged on Jud's serene face. I kept singing, and he kept smiling. It was incredible! Then he began to seem sleepy again.

I decided to read to him from his toddler Bible. His favorite story has long been the story of Job (see journal entry from 6/27/2007: Jud's Vision), but it wasn't until I read the story of "Baby Jesus"[24] that Jud's eyes suddenly popped open, as if he had just awoken from a long slumber, and his countenance was profoundly raised; he began engaging with me—lucid. It was special.

I quickly went and awoke Drake from his sleep, and the two of us enjoyed a beautiful, sweet time with Jud. He has not since had a lucid/conscious moment, but his smiles from Monday morning are seared in my mind and heart forever.

Letter 56: Wednesday, November 7

Our dear family and friends,

We ushered Judson into the arms of Jesus around 11:30 a.m. this morning.

We do not grieve as those without hope.

In his loving embrace,
Christina, Drake, and Jessie

After Loss:
Trusting in Brokenness

* * *

Judson died in my arms that bleak Wednesday morning. I held his frail frame as he slowly breathed his last breaths then cradled his limp body, crying hysterically. I was in shock! We believed so strongly that God was going to heal Judson that we had not even discussed or planned for his death. How could this be? Weren't you going to restore him, Lord?

Even as I slowly placed his thin, lifeless frame on his Lightning McQueen sheets for the last time, I could not help but think that God was going to breathe new life into his body. This could not possibly be the end!

Drake and I took time to clean his motionless frame, changing his diaper for the last time and dressing him in a red and navy striped polo shirt, and my favorite Quicksilver shorts that I had picked up for him at the thrift store long before he was big enough to fit them. Then I gently placed his favorite blanket in the crook of his arm and sat there staring at his still, colorless face.

Judson's Toddler Bible[25] was lying nearby, and I suddenly felt strangely compelled to pick it up and read our little man's favorite story aloud.

"One day a man ran to Job. 'Your children and animals have died,' he said. Then Job got sores all over him," I said, choking out each word. "Did Job get angry at God? No! 'God gave me all I had,' said Job. 'I will still love him.'"

"Judson, you are the one who epitomized Job," I declared in between sobs to the dead boy beside me. "You suffered so much, and yet you lived with such joy. You loved God well in your little life. We are so proud of you! I want to honor you by loving God in *our* suffering too."

Letter 57: Thursday, November 8

Dear family, friends, and friends we have never met who have walked this journey alongside us,

The Memorial Service for Judson will be:

> Monday, November 12, 3:00 p.m.
> Evangelical Free Church Of Fullerton

We would be blessed to have you there.

Much gratitude,
Christina and Drake

Letter 58: Friday, November 9

Dearest family and friends (sent only to our closest friends and family),

Judson's Burial Service will be:

> Tuesday, November 13, 10:30 a.m
> Fairhaven Memorial Park & Mortuary
> Edgewood Garden, Plot 7G

We also invite you to join us for lunch afterward at Danielle and Marty's home.

Furthermore, as Judson's Memorial Service approaches, we have a strong desire to worship the Lord with all of you ahead of time and ask him to bless and speak through the commemoration. We marvel at how God has used our Jud in the lives of many people through this circumstance and are hopeful that God will use Jud's service to further his glory. You have directly contended alongside us for Jud over these months; will you join us in praise and prayer on Sunday night to the end that God may be glorified as we honor our boy's life the next day?

Love you all so much,
Drake and Christina

Monday, November 12

Memorial Service Quotes and Reflection

How do you measure a life? In years? In accomplishments? In diplomas? In material wealth? Deep down most of us know that those things are not good measures of a life. And yet as I struggled to make sense of what was happening to Judson, I struggled most with the fact that he was so young. Too young, I felt, for this to befall him. "For goodness sake, he's not even three?" But over time I saw things with different lenses: I saw God at work in the lives of so many; I saw worship, praise, and confession. I saw the Spirit softening hearts and changing minds. I sensed the Spirit softening my heart and changing my mind. And I eventually realized that our lives should only appropriately be measured by God's hand on them. Is he glorified in and through our lives? With that as our measure, then I say Jud lived a full and fruitful life.

Mark Page, family friend and pastor

* * *

Thinking back to the memorial service (viewable online at www.StoryOfJudson.com), it still feels unreal. Over eight hundred people gathered on Veteran's Day to join us in honoring the life of our precious boy. His little casket, surrounded by flowers, pictures, and some of his toys graced the front of the church as various people, along with Drake and I, shared stories of Jud, described his character, and spoke of his impact.

* * *

I was so blessed to get to see Jud nearly every day, and his mommy and daddy will tell you that I was Judson's "first best friend." He was pretty little when we realized that he was very smart and so obedient—always such a joy. I am so thankful for all of the wonderful memories I have with him. Hearing his first words, seeing his first steps, celebrating his birthday, and knowing what a loving, sweet-natured little guy he was … Jud might not have lived long enough to learn reading, writing and arithmetic, but one thing is for certain: he knew Jesus, and he knew that Jesus loved him.

June Catron, family friend and neighbor

* * *

Jud with his smile, and his beauty, reached out and stole my heart, and now I am forever changed … My best model of God's strength was in this precious boy who was losing his abilities, and his body was so weak. What

many of you may not know is all the things
Jud still could do in his last months and weeks.

Jud and I swam in the ocean with Dori, looking
for Nemo. We went to the zoo and roared with
the lions. We ran from dogs in the park and
raced up the stairs to the longest slide in the
world, and then I watched as he went down,
while I blew gently on his forehead so he felt
the wind. Although we could sit in a room full
of toys, nothing sustained Jud more than his
memories and imagination ... Jud appreciated
the simple pleasures. He appreciated laughter,
a good joke, and a smile. God has entered my
life before and has changed me, and through
this little boy I am forever changed as well.

Sarah Hegenbart Bobar,
family friend and Judson's caregiver

●　　●　　●

I cried, wept, and even laughed at the sweet reflections
of our beloved son, yet all the while feeling as though
my reality had been suspended and this could not actually be happening. As we delighted in videos of Jud and
sang some of his favorite songs describing the goodness
of our Lord, it was contrasted with a genuine wrestling
over the Lord's decision not to heal our little man.

●　　●　　●

As Krabbe disease progressed, our faith grew,
and we began to hope and expect that Judson
would be healed. Many of you stood with us
in the same type of faith—with extraordinary
prayer, offered at all hours, and with fast-

ing … Why haven't we received the answer we expected? I don't know. We may never know why God has not answered our faith-filled prayers for Judson's healing here on earth. But I do know this: I still believe the God I serve hears the prayers of His people. There's one prayer that we have always prayed for Jud that God has answered in extraordinary ways. We've prayed, for as long as we have had Jud, that God would make him a blessing. If today's celebration of his life is any indication, then God has made our Judson a blessing not only to us but to many people.

Drake Levasheff

•   •   •

Drake and Christina, and in a lesser way those who believed with them, have taken a terrible risk. They have risked believing that God would do something that he clearly has not. They risked asking God for something he did not give. And they risked asking for it publicly … And now their grief is public too. But what has also been made public is a proper view of who God is. They have risked behaving in such a way that if Jesus were alive and walking around today they would do everything in their power to get their son in front of him and beg him to heal Jud. And why should they, or we, not behave in such a way? They behaved as if God is good, God is powerful, God is a healer, God is a Father who loves them and listens to the prayers of his children. They risked behaving with a proper view of who God is. They believed that God is not a God who asks

us to come to him with watered-down hopes.
Of all people we ought to hope…

Craig and Kelly Hill, family friends

⚬   ⚬   ⚬

Moved by every word spoken, I, too, had the opportunity to share. And as I approached the podium to offer a short ten-minute eulogy, it felt extremely inadequate to express the depths of my feelings and love for my son, along with my anguish over his death. I found myself almost detached from the experience, hovering above as I stared at the hundreds of people with tear-stained eyes, words flowing from my lips:

> Judson had so many qualities. Amongst the many, he was a teacher; he had a teacher's heart. As he soaked in the world around him, he also wanted to help others learn. He frequently pointed out to Jessie various objects around our home. He would ask, "Can you say, Chevy Blazer?" while placing his Match-box Chevy Blazer in Jessie's hand. A favorite teaching moment was when he was eating a banana and said, "Jessie, can you say banana—BA-NAN-NA. BA-NAN-NA. Jessie, can you say that?"

> Judson's teaching will not stop. I will spend the rest of my life reflecting on his couple years, knowing there is so much to learn from him. Not only am I honored and extremely proud to have been Jud's mom, but I am also blessed to be his student.

Stepping off the stage, I walked across the floor, passing the mahogany stained casket where the small body of my first child, my only boy, my beloved buddy lay, and the thought kept racing through my mind, "How do I possibly live now? How do I live without my Judson? How do I do this?"

Journal Entry: Thursday, November 15

Joy in the Morning

Eight days without Jud ...

> Weeping may endure for a night, but joy comes
> in the morning.
>
> *Psalm* 30:5

When I woke the next morning after Jud died, I didn't want to open my eyes. I lay in bed, motionless, broken, my mind scrambling to understand the heartache in my soul. It felt unreal. Could my Mr. Handsome actually be gone from this life forever? How do I live in this intense grief?

Drake got Jessie up and brought her into our bed. She began climbing on both of us, laughing, rolling around, playing with my belly button, making kissing noises, and "talking."

As Jessie playfully carried on, Drake and I shared some of our confusion and feelings.

"In a circumstance where severe suffering leads to death, and now we must live with the intense grief of losing our son, how is it possible for joy to come in the morning?" I asked, longing for comfort in our sorrow.

Drake rolled Jessie over toward me, and as she giggled with glee, he responded, "Jessie is your joy in the morning. She is our joy!"

238

Profound, yet so simple. Yes, indeed! Jessie is our joy in the morning, afternoon, and evening. She is such a joy!

This realization reminded me that I must daily choose to have eyes that see the grace, joy, hope, peace, and love in our circumstance. It is a conscious decision to find the beauty in sorrow rather than allow the darkness to consume.

Today I woke up, again not wanting to open my eyes. The loss of Jud is surreal. I am broken, trying to understand the heartache in my soul. The anguish over losing Jud will persist—pain with each conscious breath.

However, with every day of sorrow I will also look for the "joy in the morning." Whether it is Jessie or Drake or the flowers sitting outside my door or the phone call from a friend, I will consciously choose to find the joy.

Journal Entry: Friday, November 16

Death Delivered Life

Nine days without Jud...

Though we know that death here on earth is inevitable for everyone, it still seems strangely foreign, often shrouded in troublesome mystery. However, Judson's recent passing has tangibly reminded me of the very real hope that death can be synonymous with life.

Judson's last morning here on earth was, unfortunately, filled with tremendous suffering, even though we did everything we could to keep him comfortable. Our hearts felt like they were being ripped out of our chests as we watched our precious boy struggle to breathe—I have never seen such profound physical agony and pain in such a young body (not even in movies). Therein, I found myself deeply torn; I longed to see Judson set free and relieved from such tremendous affliction, but I also knew that meant no longer being able to hold his warm body, kiss his beautiful face, and whisper my love in his ear.

In an effort to catch my own breath, I stepped away for a moment of solitude and fell against our bathroom wall, weeping. My back slid down the olive-painted surface as I crumbled to the floor in distress. Overcome by heartache, I cried out to God, "I don't know how to walk this path! How do I encourage Jud to let go so he can be set free when I desperately don't want to lose him? Oh Father, how do I walk this impossible path?" I just kept sobbing, my heart and mind clouded in anguish.

I didn't want to go back in Jud's room to endure more of his pain with him, but I also could not stay away—constantly conflicted. I finally rejoined my family, snuggling up to Drake and Jud on our beanbag chair. Jud's breathing had calmed. I continued to weep, all the while wondering, How do I walk this path?

A few moments later, life came upon us; Jessie rushed into the room, laughing, dancing, and smiling. In her innocence, completely unaware of the heartache surrounding her, she brought amusement and delight.

Judson was experiencing death and dying, while Jessie reflected life and living.

As I watched her parade around the room in happiness, I knew God was giving me the strength to let go of my sweet man. More than my desire to hold and care for him, I desperately wanted Jud to experience life anew, to be able to laugh and dance again, just like his baby sister.

I turned and gently whispered in his ear, "Judson, I love you so much. I am so proud of you. You are the bravest boy I know. You've been such a fighter, but you can let go now. Run into the arms of Jesus; he loves you so much! I will miss you more than you can imagine, but it won't be long until I see you again. You can let go, Bud Bud. Find peace and rest." My tears dripped onto his cheek.

It wasn't long after that my Jud the Stud breathed his last breath and died, but in that same moment, he found life once more—running, dancing, singing, laughing, and praising God.

Thank you, Lord, that because of your Son's suffering, death delivered Judson unto life again!

Journal Entry: Sunday, November 18

It Did Not Disappoint

Eleven days without Jud...

I really believed God was going to heal Jud here on earth.

When we first received word that Judson had an incurable, terminal disease, I remember thinking it felt too risky to believe that God could heal Jud—what if I hope, and God chooses not to heal him? Won't my pain be greater?

I hoped, and God chose not to heal Jud.

I wouldn't change a thing.

It is hope that strengthened me to walk Jud's path of suffering. It is hope that enabled me to release him into the hands of Jesus. It is because of hope that I have no regrets.

Hope did not disappoint.

I still have questions, confusion, and immeasurable pain, but I trust the God of all hope.

Journal Entry: Wednesday, November 28

Why Not?

Twenty-one days without Jud...

We frequently have people assume that Drake and I are asking the questions, *Why, God? Why us? Why Jud? Why have you allowed us to walk this path of pain and suffering?* If these questions are founded in a belief that we somehow do not deserve this affliction, then this query does not sit well with me.

It appears that inherent in these particular questions is a sense of entitlement. The underlying tenet seems to assume that one somehow believes their challenges in life are not justified or that God has given them a situation that is not fair.

I am not entitled to anything. Our lives are a gift, and all that we have been given is a gift. We are not guaranteed a pain-free existence. Though it can be horribly trying, pain is part of living in a fallen world.

Moreover, the question of *Why, God?* also appears void of gratitude. When we believe we don't deserve our pain on the life journey we've been given, then it can be difficult to be thankful for the blessings that have been bestowed upon us. Discontentment breeds ingratitude.

Conversely, gratitude breeds contentment.

I want a heart that maintains a grateful posture despite external circumstances. Ultimately I have been given a gift that far outweighs the pains of this temporal existence—I have been given the hope of eternity with the Author and Creator of the universe, where pain will be no more, along now with the promise that my son awaits me there.

Journal Entry: Monday, December 3

God is Not a Genie

Twenty-six days without Jud...

Recently someone asked me this question: "After praying with faith for Judson's healing and having God choose not to heal, will you ever be able to pray in faith again for God to miraculously heal?"

"I hope so," I responded, much to their dismay.

I am learning that prayer is not about getting what you want; God is not a genie. Prayer is about recognizing God for who he is, being obedient to petition him in all things, acknowledging his complete power, and standing on the truths of his Word. Prayer causes us to press in to our Father and develops our relationship with him.

Prayer is also a tangible way to love. We had so many people offering faith-filled prayers for God to miraculously heal Jud, and it was such an incredible act of love toward us. We were touched by it, and I believe that all who prayed in faith were moved as well. Submissive yet expectant prayer changes lives.

God answered our collective prayers for Jud to be healed here on earth with a resounding no when he took Jud into his presence on November 7, 2007. Though the pain is excruciating with this answer, a surrendered heart accepts the answers from God Almighty, who knows the end from the beginning and is working all things out for the good of those who love him. Prayer trusts.

Lastly, I believe with all my being that the same Jesus who healed and raised the dead when he walked this earth is still moving in miraculous ways today. I perceive that when we read about the power of our Lord as described in Scripture, it often falls flat because we, particularly in our Western culture during this age, have not tangibly experienced God moving in these ways. I want to. I want to see God rain down his kingdom power here on earth.

So, yes, the next time I am invited to pray in faith for someone to be miraculously healed, I hope I can expectantly enter in, recognizing it as a means to love them, trusting in the character of my Father, hoping to deepen my relationship with Jesus, and desiring to see the Holy Spirit move in a fresh and mighty way. I consider it a privilege that I can partner with the Creator of all through prayer.

Journal Entry: Wednesday, December 5

Wrestling

One month without Jud...

In my journal titled "Raw Moments" from September 16, 2007, I described my fears that I was believing God to heal Jud, yet he could still die. At the end of the post, I described how I spelled out the word trust in the steam on the windshield of our car that night.

Now, here I am, on the other side. Jud died. My greatest fears came to fruition.

Our faith has definitely been tested, and I have had moments of wrestling with God, particularly out of confusion. Beyond just having faith for God to heal Jud, I actually believed God's "still, small voice" was making it known to us that he did, in fact, intend to heal Jud here on earth.

Yet he did not.

How do I reconcile this?

A couple things Drake recently shared in a note were an epiphany for me as I have struggled to understand how God was speaking.

> How could we misunderstand God when we felt like he was speaking so clearly to us? The critical problem I faced during this period was that I had spent too little of my life trying to hear God's voice. These times of listening have been confined to my own life crises—and so (sadly) I'm not as attuned to the Spirit as I need to be.

As I look back now, I remember situations where God may

have been trying to communicate with me that he was going to take Jud, but I am not adept at listening to his voice, and it is not what I wanted to hear, so I could not receive it at the time.

> Another thing that happened is that I began to confuse hope with God's voice. It is right for us to hope, but that doesn't mean that we will always receive from God what we hope for—no matter how good we know it could be. I know there were times that I and others spoke and prayed with hope, but on many occasions I confused this with God's direction.

I certainly confused hope with God's voice. I wanted so badly for God to heal Jud that I saw everything through that lens. In fact, it got to the point where I could see nothing else, and anything that might direct me otherwise, I squelched. We are called to prayer in faith and hope, but that does not equate to God's intentions.

All the nuances of faith baffle me, and I certainly have significant need for growth, but God has been gracious and loving toward us through this process, especially in our shortcomings. He sees our frailties and cares for us nonetheless.

As Drake and I were driving in our car this evening, after discussing many issues of faith with our friends, the windows in our car began to steam up. Suddenly, the word trust began to appear on our windshield. I looked at it in awe, remembering the night I had written it. I stared at it for several minutes, surprised that I had not seen it any other time in the three months since I wrote it. It served as a wonderful reminder that in all things, even my wrestling with God, the bottom line is that I have been called to trust.

Trusting still sits well with my soul.

Journal Entry: Thursday, January 10, 2008

Metamorphosis

Two months without Jud...

This journey with Judson has led to a transformation in my faith, and I have been pondering the depths of this change.

Herein lies my metamorphosis.

Prior to the onset of Jud's illness, I felt like my faith consisted of solid belief, but it was a belief coupled with cynicism about the evangelical church in the United States. Over time, I had observed inconsistencies in espoused beliefs versus how the church interacted with and treated the world. I was put off by some of the legalism that often seemed to go hand-in-hand with the believing population, and I had been hurt by some of the ways I had experienced Christians treating one another. I began to want to distance myself from Christian culture.

But the rubber met the road, in terms of my faith, at the time Jud got ill. My belief system was significantly tested. Whether or not I wanted to be associated with the evangelical Christian culture, this was the moment of truth. In the deepest and darkest moments of my life, would that which I had believed about God, his character, and his Word ring true? Would there be a consistency in the faith I had professed for much of my life when my world came crashing down around me?

The reality is that this wretched, heinous disease called Krabbe made the existence of a loving yet almighty God undeniably real in my life. His Word came alive. His character proved dependable. And yet his ways remained mysterious. My faith became linked to my experience of God.

Furthermore, this evangelical church in the United States that had triggered cynicism in my heart touched our lives in an incredible way. God mobilized his people to love, and I am humbled that we have been recipients of such astounding compassion and grace.

But where Judson's illness tested my belief, Judson's death causes me to bank on that belief every single day. Every truth of Scripture now has intimate ramifications for my life. All spiritual songs carry greater depth of meaning. If not for the death and resurrection of Jesus Christ, evil Krabbe would have triumphed over our family in the death of our son. But because of Jesus, there is the promise of hope; I remind myself with each breath here on earth that I am drawing closer to a life in eternity, where I will be reunited with my son and set free from the suffering that had become synonymous with Judson's life and is now a way of life for me. I don't just believe it; I am staking my very existence on it.

Sunday, January 13

Excerpts from a Sermon **by Drake Levasheff**

As soon as we found out that Judson had Krabbe disease, it became evident to us that treating it was beyond medicine's reach because the disease had progressed so quickly for him. Once we came to that realization, we began to look to the Lord and to hope in him for Jud's healing. Soon after that, I became very aware of how "out there" we were. I began to see the concern and trepidation in people's faces. Many—believers and unbelievers alike—wondered how we could hope to accomplish in prayer what was outside of the reach of medical science. Judson had been given a death sentence. Shouldn't we just have accepted our fate and avoided the embarrassment?

Even now, I embrace the decision we made to hope and pray for Jud's healing and to reject society's conventional wisdom. Though the result was not what we wanted, Jesus commends this way of approaching God in prayer, asking with boldness and without shame.

But what are we to say when we ask God, as we are taught, for good and needful things and yet don't receive the answer we seek? Why would the Scripture teach us "ask and you shall receive" (John 15 and 16), but in many cases the answer we seek boldly never comes?

We've thought long and hard about this in light of our loss of Judson. There was so much prayer for him, so much asking done so boldly with so much faith by so many people at all hours. We thought so much glory and good could come to God from Jud's deliverance from a disease that only he could heal. But after praying and hoping boldly for months, we are left with our memories of Jud and our grief, which threatens to engulf us ...

If we conclude that God still heals miraculously today (which we, in fact, still do), it gets hard, for we're left to say that God can and does heal, but he decided not to heal Jud here on earth. Why didn't God answer our prayers? Are we to believe what Jesus says when he declares, "Ask and it will be given to you?" (Luke 11:9, NASB)

Here is what I know with certainty to be true: that we pray to one who comes to us as a Father and gives us good gifts. It's tempting to read Scripture a certain way; we read "ask and it will be given to you" (Luke 11:9, NASB) and expect that if we ask for something good and we fulfill our end of the deal that we're always going to get what we asked for. But God is not an ATM machine; he's a person. And prayer isn't about putting in a card and entering the right code as though if I don't get what I ask, I must have put in the wrong code. It's about an ongoing relationship with a person. Lucky for us, we call him Father, and even if he doesn't always do what we ask, we can still trust him to give good gifts. And that is something we can rest in. That's something I can rest in...

Journal Entry: Sunday, April 6

Does Not Nullify

Five months without Jud...

Seeing as we prayed so fervently for God to heal Jud, and he obviously did not, I have spent a lot of time pondering how God might have been responding as we were begging him to restore our son's body to wholeness—something he clearly did not plan to do.

It would be easy for me to perceive that he cavalierly and without emotion brushed aside our requests, knowing he did not intend to heal our boy. There are times such thoughts race through my mind, but these pictures spring from view- ing God as an indifferent or even heartless ruler or dicta- tor who delights in his exercise of power without regard for his subjects. If this is the God I serve, then my faith would certainly now be destroyed—the death of my son would be indicative of a God without love.

Others may suggest that God is actually distant and removed from this world; he no longer intervenes in the lives of his creation. Thoughts such as this nullify the need for prayer altogether, making our pursuit of God ludicrous and our requests for healing an absurd concept. If this is the God I serve, then my faith equates to foolishness.

But based on the character of God portrayed in Scripture, I have another picture that forms my faith. It is shaped by God's response to his beloved Son when Jesus asked, in anguish, for his Father to "remove this cup" from him. The

Son of God was about to suffer and die, and as much as the Father deeply loved him, heard his cries, felt his pain, and had the power to save him, the Father denied his Son's request because there was a larger plan involved. God did not kill his own son, but he allowed it to happen and used it for the redemption of man.

Similarly, I trust that our requests for Jud to be healed here on earth were heard by a loving Father who felt our pain deeply. I imagine him looking upon us with such compassion as we petitioned him. I expect he was pleased that we acknowledged his power to heal but was also tremendously sad knowing he was not going to intervene. Though he had the ability to heal Jud from Krabbe, a disease he did not cause but allowed to happen, his choice not to restore our little man to health is part of a plan that is much larger than our broken hearts. And as much as it hurts, it does not nullify his love.

Of course, God's decision not to heal Jud is still extremely hard for me to swallow, but it does not equate to him being distant or heartless toward our cries. On the other hand, though his love is rich, I am realizing he is not as concerned about our lives being free of pain in this lifetime as he is about wanting us to surrender to his larger plan for eternity.

Even in my brokenness, I want to surrender.

Journal Entry: Tuesday, April 22

Wounded by a Trusted Friend

Five and a half months without Jud...

I've been wounded by a trusted friend.

It was not malicious. It was not vindictive. It was not out

of spite. It was not because of displeasure or disfavor. It was neither out of anger nor frustration.

I've been deeply wounded by my most trusted friend, when he did what he actually thought was best.

I've been wounded by God.

It would be disingenuous to deny these wounds. God hurt me profoundly when he did not heal Judson. To know he had the power to intervene and give Jud back to us but chose not to is more painful than words. I came to God and gave him one of my most beloved treasures, requesting that he give my precious child back to me, restored to health, but instead he turned and walked away with my boy in his arms, leaving my arms empty and my heart broken.

My deepest and most intense wounds came from my most trusted friend.

In that manner, do these wounds affect my relationship with God? Of course! How can they not? In any relationship, when one has been wounded, it has an impact; the dynamics cannot help but be influenced by the pain.

So does God remain my most trusted friend?

Absolutely! The same God whose character was the foundation of our hope for Jud's healing is worthy of my trust for that exact reason: his character. God has proven faithful in my life. I know his love and care for me; I have experienced it firsthand.

Just as my relationship with Drake has yielded wounds at times when he has done what he believed was best, it does not change my love for him. Why? Because I know Drake; I know his character. I know he is an honorable man who strives to live uprightly. It is Drake's character (though fallible at times too) that enables me to continue to love and trust him despite any wounds from him.

Moreover, I know God's infallible character. I know he is a good and loving God. I also know that I am a finite being with limited understanding; he is the infinite, almighty God who knows the end from the beginning. His perspective on Jud's situation had to take into account much more that just my feelings—he did not want to hurt me in doing what he saw as best, though he knew it would. Yet despite God's decision, I sense that his heart of compassion broke with mine and continues to grieve with me over the loss of Judson on this earth (just as he grieves all the effects of evil in this world but does not necessarily intervene).

Though God's decision not to heal Jud has inflicted immeasurable sorrow and lifelong wounds, I continue to love and trust him, because I know he is worthy of my trust.

Journal Entry: Monday, April 28

Misinterpretation

Almost six months without Jud...

One afternoon, when Judson was about eight months old, he was crying uncontrollably, and as I rocked him back and forth, I felt like God whispered in my ear, "Judson is special. I have great plans for him but I will care for him. He is special" (see Meet Judson).

As these words echoed in my heart, I found huge comfort and encouragement for the moment, but I also understood them to mean neat and exciting things for the future. In my limited understanding, I interpreted what God expressed to me through my finite, distorted lens.

I sheepishly admit that I thought God might have been planning something spectacular for my Jud Bud. With the word special, I envisioned God hand-selecting Jud and setting him apart for "great plans" to be a very influential adult in this world. When God said he would "care for" Jud, I visualized Jud's protection from harm and evil and his basic needs being met throughout his life.

But God was communicating something diametrically different to me.

Yes, indeed, God had something spectacular planned for Jud, but not impressive by the worlds standards. Judson is "special" because he was set apart to walk a journey of pain and suffering that few endure. God had "great plans" to use Jud's short life as a testimony for the kingdom, and when the Lord said he would "care for" Jud, he meant literally, not figuratively—I am no longer taking care of my little man; God is.

I truly believe God spoke to me, but I heard his words through my skewed understanding and desires. In many ways, I took his words to mean what I wanted them to mean.

I have a lot to learn about understanding God's still, small voice.

Journal Entry: Monday, May 5

Petitions

Half a year without Jud ...

I am struggling with offering faith-filled petitions to my Father.

When Judson first died, I remember thinking that though our request for Jud's healing on earth was denied, I would not have difficulty praying in faith for other various circumstances. Unfortunately, this has proven far more challenging than I expected.

It is not that my general prayer life has been stunted; I am often desperate to converse with God, but I am reticent to petition him for anything wherefore I will know whether or not my prayer has been answered.

I'm afraid.

I'm afraid of being hurt and disappointed.

I came to my Father with the most significant request I expect I will ever make, partly out of obedience, and he painfully said no. Therefore, it is a fear of more pain that has been keeping me from requesting anything else of him; he might say no again, and I'm not sure I can handle more disappointment.

Correspondingly, if I had approached my earthly dad with a meaningful request of significant value that I actually perceived he wanted me to ask of him, and then he denied my request, I would feel deflated and hesitant to make further requests. My spirit feels similarly dejected and broken.

Yet, if I never again ask the Lord for anything, then it is impossible to taste the life-changing movement of his hand that can be experienced through answered prayer. Furthermore, we are called to make our requests known to him, to engage him at our deepest level of need.

So what do I do?

Well, first and foremost, I think he understands. I don't think God expects much more of me right now than to be honest and forthright about these difficulties. And just as I would do with my dad in the above hypothetical situation, I talk with God about my struggles and lack of understanding.

I tell him my fears. I ask him to help me regain the trust necessary to beseech his intervention in this dark world. I also remind myself of the many prayers he has previously answered in my life, especially those that can be explained only by the work of his hand.

Therefore, with what little faith I can muster, I pray that over time even my prayer life will begin to heal.

Journal Entry: Friday, June 13

Indelible Reminder

Seven months without Jud...

Just a couple hours after Judson died, I crumbled on my bed and wept and wept and wept. The book *Morning by Morning* by Charles Spurgeon[26] happened to be sitting on my nightstand staring me in the face, so I decided to pick it up and read the entry for that day, November 7. What I read has remained emblazoned in my mind and continues to be one of my greatest sources of comfort as I have grieved the loss of my boy.

Spurgeon described how in the book of Isaiah, Zion is feeling abandoned by God and declares, "The Lord hath forsaken me, and my Lord hath forgotten me" (Isaiah 49:14, KJV).

There have been many moments in the last year where I have been tempted toward unbelief and feelings of being deserted by God, but the Lord's loving word of admonition offered to the disbelieving people of Zion keeps ringing in my mind.

> Behold, I have graven thee upon the palms of
> my hands.
>
> *Isaiah* 49:16 KJV

He is declaring his constant faithfulness and the impossibility for him to forget his beloved; he has even gone so far as to etch them into his own skin.

So I took a bold step today, on the anniversary when our souls began to cry out in brokenness for the life of our boy— the day marking the subsequent slow and painful death of our precious Judson, along with the dying that has occurred in our hearts.

I have inscribed Jud's name on my wrist.

Each painful stroke as Judson was "memorialized in my flesh" felt like an appropriate reflection of the blistering sorrow in my soul, but as the emotion of the occasion apprehended my heart, I meditated over and over on this verse from Isaiah.

> Behold, I have graven thee upon the palms of
> my hands.
>
> *Isaiah* 49:16 KJV

Just as I have etched Judson on my wrist as a symbol that he can never be forgotten, so also has my Father carved me into his hand. He cannot and will not forsake me. He is faithful and he is good. I am never to be forgotten by the One who created me.

This lifelong decision to have Jud's name written on my body in such a prominent location carries great weight: possible stigma, possible change in first impressions, or a possible mischaracterization of intentions, but the symbolism far outweighs the costs for me.

I have an indelible reminder of God's promise of faithfulness and my promise to never forget Jud.

Journal Entry: Thursday, June 26

Miraculous Healing

Seven and a half months without Jud...

I've been reading a book that describes in detail someone's experience of God answering prayers for one man's miraculous healing.

I must admit it's been hard for me.

As much as I would like to say that this story quickens my heart in hope to see God move in profoundly supernatural ways, it has done the opposite for me. It has left me wondering why God did not answer the thousands of Spirit-filled prayers for Judson to be healed and remain on earth as a testimony of God's miraculous power.

It hurts.

God could have healed Jud. He did not.

It hurts.

I don't question his omniscient plans, because my understanding is so limited, and I certainly want to submit to his desires for me/us, believing in his goodness, but it doesn't minimize the intense hurt.

God heals some. He did not heal Jud.

It hurts.

Journal Entry: Friday, October 17

What If?

Eleven months without Jud...

Last year on October 14, our home was filled with people coming from near and far to love on Jud. We had an open house to give people who had been following his story the opportunity to be with him in person—those who had met him before, and those who had not.

Over 120 people crammed into our little townhome that afternoon; we chatted, ate, sang, prayed, cried, and more. Jud soaked in all the attention from everyone even though he couldn't see the faces of the many people who looked upon him with tremendous love.

But we saw it and were so blessed by it!

At the time, Judson's body was clearly starting to show signs of critical dysfunction. As I recall the last-minute decision to host the open house for Jud, there were many issues at play, including allowing people to see him and say goodbye should he pass away. But there was also an unstated motive that now seems so crazy in light of Judson's death but at the time was on our minds too.

We had strong belief that God was going to heal our son. So in light of this belief, and in recognition of the fact that we expected there would be many doubters and nay-sayers were God to heal Jud, part of our intention with the open house was actually to have as many witnesses as possible who could attest to the severity of Judson's condition and then later proclaim God's mighty power made evident in the body of our sweet boy.

But God didn't intervene. Instead, we realized just a few

weeks later that these visitors had been, in fact, saying their goodbyes to Jud.

It has been almost a year now since Judson's last breath, and our faith for his earthly healing continues to be a point of contemplation for me.

Does God intervene supernaturally in this world now? If yes, why did God choose not to heal Jud? How does one understand his leading and know if they are actually hearing his still, small voice? What is the purpose of calling us to unwavering faith if not to see the object of our faith realized? How do I have sincere faith for anything else after this incredible heartache? And ultimately, what is the purpose of all this? What is the point?

Though I am still very much at a loss for most of these answers, I am slowly gaining more clarity in some of the haze of these and other questions, which has led me to another question.

What if God had healed Jud?

Of course, it would have been an incredible manifestation of his supernatural power, and the Lord might have used it significantly for his kingdom. However, were I to speculate, I actually think a ministry of triumph in this manner may not be as relevant to most people as is a ministry of suffering; Drake and I want our story (Jud's story) to be a ministry.

I would imagine Judson's healing would have been met with much speculation and assuredly an inability for most to relate. People might be encouraged by the story, but I'm not sure they would personally connect to the story. They might conclude that it is easy to trust God in triumph but still speculate whether or not we would have trusted God in our affliction had there been no "happy" ending.

So many people are hurting. I think particularly of the relationships I have been building electronically and in person with other women who have or are losing their children to Krabbe. Had God healed Judson, they would probably want little or nothing to do with me. They would be unable to relate and likely wonder with disparagement why God healed Jud but not their child? Our story would not be relevant to them.

I also wonder had God healed Jud, would we have our current relationship with a dear couple from church who has been in financial turmoil while the husband is simultaneously losing his battle with cancer? Doubtful. Would we be getting calls to meet with families who have lost children? Unlikely. Would we have a ministry to people who are struggling? Maybe, but they might find it difficult to relate to us.

In fact, our story would probably not be relevant to many had God healed Jud. Why? Because people are suffering on every corner in this world, and I am beginning to see that faith becomes particularly profound when it is upheld at severe cost; it is not hard to have faith when it costs you very little, but faith in hardship is weighty.

Why am I so confident in this premise? Because right now I am the one deeply hurting, and the people who are having the greatest impact in my life are those who have also suffered, those who know pain, those who question God in their affliction yet maintain a heart that still longs to trust their heavenly Father.

Oh, how I wish that I and our visitors on October 14 last year had never needed to say goodbye to my little man, and I may never fully understand why God didn't heal Judson until I am reunited with my beloved boy. But in the meantime, I hope my Father will foster in me a heart of surrender that might lead others toward spiritual healing through Jesus Christ due, in part, to the unrestored earthly body of my son.

God may not have healed Jud, but I hope he heals many hearts through Jud.

Journal Entry: Tuesday, December 16

Five-letter Word

One year and one month without Jud...

I am embarrassed to admit that the inside windshield of our car has not been washed in over a year. How do I know?

I can only count a handful of times when I have seen it, but the other night, the word trust that I scribbled onto our foggy windshield back in September 2007 (see Raw Moments and Wrestling) became visible to me once again. How it eludes my attention most of the time, I do not know. However, each time this five-letter word scrawled in the corner of the window of our sedan catches my eye, I am profoundly moved.

"Trust," glaring in the moonlight, is a direct and tangible reminder of the constant challenge of my life. When nothing seems to make sense, when the pain is massive, when the strain of sorrow threatens every aspect of my being, I am called to trust my heavenly Father.

Trust that God loves me even when my boy died. Trust that he cares about my future and has a unique plan for my life. Trust that he tenderly holds my broken heart and has a purpose for this pain. Trust that his ways are ultimately good, drawing me into depth of relationship with him. Trust that his promises are true, even when it feels like they failed me. Trust that he is indeed real, alive, active, and working in this world. Trust that the God I have surrendered my life to is, in fact, trustworthy.

This kind of trust is not easy. Maybe that's why, during intense heartache and fear, I felt strangely compelled to carefully draw T-R-U-S-T into the steam on our windshield that night. God knew it would serve as a powerful reminder to lean not on my own understanding and simply trust him (Proverbs 3:5).

Epilogue

* * *

We truly believed God was going to heal Judson. Even right up to the day he died, we remained hopeful. However, healing Jud here on earth was clearly not God's design for our son. So what do we make of this journey of faith, and these confident prayers that resulted in an undesirable answer from our heavenly Father?

We are still in deep grief over the loss of our precious boy—much has yet to be revealed to us, and many questions may remain unanswered; but there are a few thoughts that keep me grounded in my ability to see God in our heart-wrenching disappointment.

First of all, I have an abiding sense that the Lord was and is very pleased with our faith, even though he did not heal Judson as we had hoped and believed. During this season, we scoured his Word, immersed ourselves in worship, and ultimately hung our faith on the person of Jesus Christ and the character of God. Our faith was not in the actual healing, though we desperately longed for it; our faith was in the Giver of life and breath. We did not accept the death sentence given by doctors, mortal man, as the final word for our son; we recognized God as the Great Healer yesterday, today, and forever, and placed our beloved boy in his arms as best we knew how. I perceive that God was honored by this kind of faith.

Second, this circumstance put us at the mercy of our Maker, causing us and many others to earnestly press in to God in a way we would not have were we not believing him to heal. Our family was surrounded by intercessors who regularly attested to the fact that they had never before prayed so fervently for anything in their lives (we were certainly humbled by this). The Spirit of God was clearly at work in our faith-filled prayers. Calling out to my Father in need and even desperation deepened my relationship with him. I am thankful for the foundational work that was being developed through this painful journey, particularly a more prayer-filled life, one of ongoing communication with the one who calls me beloved.

Third, I have no regrets. I do not look back on the situation and wonder whether I might have done more. I was hesitant, at first, to hope and trust, but I am so thankful that I eventually stepped out in faith even when I was afraid. Had I not risked believing, I might be questioning and second-guessing myself in the midst of my grief. Furthermore, our faith in God's ability to heal Judson strengthened me to walk the path of suffering laid before us. Hope and faith did not disappoint. I discovered that the choice to believe is never one to be regretted.

Fourth, God does things that confound us. We regularly experience situations and circumstances in life that leave us with questions. Yet it does not mean that he lacks compassion, mercy, and grace. Our Father's love for us, his children, does not keep him from doing that which will bring him the greatest glory. We may not understand his ways, but we can bank on his love.

Lastly, God may not have answered our prayers to heal Judson here on earth, but he did answer our greatest prayer for our son. From the time we realized Jud was growing in my womb, we have prayed that he would be a blessing to many. It is actually through this heinous and heart-wrenching experience that the Lord has answered this prayer.

We praise Jesus that Jud is now set free from all his pain and suffering and that he is walking, leaping, and praising God in heaven. We also pray that the Lord will continue to make Judson a blessing.

Oh, how we miss our Buddy Boo!

Living with Only Shadows: Reflections in Grief

My current journal is filled with reflections and insights that I am discovering through my deep sorrow over the loss of my sweet little boy. I am being refined and shaped by this tremendous grief and yet continue to see the Lord reveal himself in big and small ways. This journey is certainly not over.

Blink

Some blink and suddenly their kids are grown.

I blinked and suddenly my son was gone.

I keep blinking.

I keep blinking, hoping my son will suddenly reappear.

He does not. He cannot in this lifetime.

A lifetime seems too long.

Yet when people are reaching the end of their days, they often express that they blinked and their life was suddenly at the closing act ...

"It moves so quickly—in the blink of an eye."

But not for me.

I can't blink fast enough to get to my son.

But one day upon closing my eyes, I will open them, and there he will be, along with other loved ones.

And when I do see him, I won't feel the pain of blinking ever again.

In the meantime, between blinks, I want eyes that glimmer with this hope.

Further Information

Please visit **www.StoryOfJudson.com** for videos of Judson and more information about Krabbe disease.

Photo courtesy of Jenny McMasters Photography
www.jennymcmastersphotography.com

Index

Month One:
My World is Crumbling

Month Two:
Crying Out in Affliction

Month Three:
Developing Unwavering Faith

Month Four:
Risking with Expectant Hope

Month Five:
Surrendering in Heartache

After Loss:
Trusting in Brokenness

Endnotes

Prologue

1   Beers, V. Gilbert. *Toddler's Bible*. Colorado Springs: Cook Communications, 2004, pp. 204–207.

Meet Judson

2   Unknown. "The Itsy Bitsy Spider or The Eensy Weensy Spider." 1962.

3   Mullins, R. Step by Step. *The World as Best as I Remember It,* 1. Brentwood: Reunion, 1991.

4   Hodges, Lynn. "B I B L E Is the Book for Me." Franklin: John T. Benson Publishing Company, 1994.

Month One:
My World is Crumbling

5   Beers, V. Gilbert. *Toddler's Bible*. Colorado Springs: Cook Communications, 2004, pp. 204–207.

6   Moreland, J. P. *Kingdom Triangle: Recover the Chris-tian Mind, Renovate the Soul, Restore the Spirit's Power.* Grand Rapids: Zondervan, 2007.

Month Two: Crying Out in Affliction

7   Chisholm, Thomas. "Great is Thy Faithfulness." 1923.

8   Rice, John R. *Praying: Asking and Receiving.* April 1948. Wheaton: Sword of the Lord, 1942, p. 84.

9   Augustine as quoted in Cowman, Charles E., Cow-man, Lettie B., Reimann, James. *Streams in the Desert.* Grand Rapids: Zondervan, 1997, p.285

10 Meyer, F. B. as quoted in Cowman, Charles E., Cow-man, Lettie B., Reimann, James. *Streams in the Desert.* Grand Rapids: Zondervan, 1997, p. 275.

11 Rice, John R. *Praying: Asking and Receiving.* April 1948. Wheaton: Sword of the Lord, 1942, p. 84.

12 Ibid.

13 Vanier, Jean. *From Brokennes to Community.* Mahwah: Paulist Press, 1992.

Month Three: Developing Unwavering Faith

14 Moreland, J. P. *Kingdom Triangle: Recover the Chris-tian Mind, Renovate the Soul, Restore the Spirit's Power.* Grand Rapids: Zondervan, 2007, p. 180.

15 Torrey, R. A. *The Power of Prayer.* Grand Rapids: Zondervan, 1987, p. 17.

16 Spurgeon, C. H. *The Power of Prayer in a Believer's Life.* Seattle: Emerald Books, 1993, p. 97.

17 Simpson, A. B. as quoted in Cowman, Charles E., Cowman, Lettie B., Reimann, James. *Streams in the Desert.* Grand Rapids: Zondervan, 1997, p. 333.

18 Willard, Dallas as quoted in Moreland, J. P. *Kingdom Triangle: Recover the Christian Mind, Renovate the Soul, Restore the Spirit's Power.* Grand Rapids: Zondervan, 2007, p. 187.

Month Four:
Risking with Expectant Hope

19 Hearn, Naida. "Jesus, Name Above All Names." Maranatha! Music, 1974.

20 Spurgeon, C. H. *Spurgeon on Prayer and Spiritual Warfare.* New Kensington: Whittaker House, 1998, p. 465.

Month Five:
Surrendering in Heartache

21 Musseau, Craig. "Arms of Love." Vineyard Publishing, 1991.

22 Deere, Jack S. *Surprised by the Voice of God.* Grand Rapids: Zondervan, 1998, p. 29.

23 Unknown. "The Itsy Bitsy Spider or The Eensy Weensy Spider." 1962.

24 Beers, V. Gilbert. *Toddler's Bible*. Colorado Springs: Cook Communications, 2004, pp. 224–227.

25 Ibid, pp. 204–208.

After Loss:
Trusting in Brokenness

26 Spurgeon, C. H. *Morning by Morning*. New Kensington: Whitaker House, 1984, p. 314.

listen|imagine|view|experience

AUDIO BOOK DOWNLOAD INCLUDED WITH THIS BOOK!

In your hands you hold a complete digital entertainment package. Besides purchasing the paper version of this book, this book includes a free download of the audio version of this book. Simply use the code listed below when visiting our website. Once downloaded to your computer, you can listen to the book through your computer's speakers, burn it to an audio CD or save the file to your portable music device (such as Apple's popular iPod) and listen on the go!

How to get your free audio book digital download:

1. Visit www.tatepublishing.com and click on the e|LIVE logo on the home page.

2. Enter the following coupon code:
   2bb5-fe1f-4214-ba3a-7f7e-447c-023c-6255

3. Download the audio book from your e|LIVE digital locker and begin enjoying your new digital entertainment package today!

CPSIA information can be obtained at www.ICGtesting.com
Printed in the USA
BVOW06s1755090416

443647BV00019B/69/P